LAW:
A Human Process

By

The Honorable Donald P. Lay

WEST GROUP

Library of Congress Cataloging-in-Publication Data

Lay, Donald P., 1926–
     Law, a human process / by Donald P. Lay.
         p.   cm.
     Includes bibliographical references.
     ISBN 0-314-20058-4 (softcover)
     1. Trial practice—United States—Anecdotes.
2. Practice of law—United States—Anecdotes.   I. Title
KF8915.Z9L37   1996
340'.023'73—dc20   96-22825
                                                                                    CIP

 PRINTED ON 10% POST CONSUMER RECYCLED PAPER

DEDICATION

This book is dedicated to Leo, Jack, John,
and Biff and "the good old days."

ABOUT THE AUTHOR

Judge Lay graduated from the University of Iowa College of Law in 1951. He practiced trial law until 1966. At that time he was appointed by President Lyndon B. Johnson to the United States Court of Appeals for the Eighth Circuit. Judge Lay became Chief Judge of the Eighth Circuit Court of Appeals in January of 1980 and served until January of 1992. From 1992-96 he served in the James A. Levee Chair as Professor of Criminal Procedure Law at the University of Minnesota. He presently serves as a Distinguished Professor of Law at William Mitchell College of Law where he teaches both civil and criminal procedure. He remains active as a Senior United States Circuit Judge and sits on the various circuit courts of appeals throughout the country.

FOREWORD

"Law: A Human Process" is a powerful text that any law student contemplating a life as an advocate or any trial lawyer will enjoy. It is not your typical how-to-do-it trial skills cookbook filled with sometimes dry prescriptions and boilerplate litany. Rather, it is a text that explores the human dimensions of the lawyering process. Its aim is to challenge the advocate to understand how the individuals within the process function. Judge Lay argues persuasively that while the trial process is surrounded "by law," the ultimate decision in any dispute turns on the interaction of the humans who are charged with its application. Understanding the human dynamics associated with the resolution of a dispute, says Judge Lay, is the most important feature of our adversarial process.

The text is based on Judge Lay's personal experience as a trial lawyer, and trial and appellate judge, which encompasses a legal career of more than 45 years. The text, which covers the trial process from complaint to verdict, is colorful, insightful, sometimes exciting, but always interesting. It should be required reading in every trial skills course in the nation and should be on the bookshelf of every trial lawyer.

Robert E. Oliphant
Professor of Law
William Mitchell College of Law

TABLE OF CONTENTS

PROLOGUE

The question many law students ask me is: "How do you become a judge?" My answer is that they must first try to become good lawyers. Non-lawyers frequently ask: "How did you happen to go to law school?" or "How did you happen to become a lawyer?"

Every lawyer has a different story. Some are more interesting than others. My story is worth telling only because it carries a message that teachers of young people should never forget. When I was in seventh grade my class divided into teams and had a debate over the merits of the French and Indian War. My social studies teacher told me afterwards that I would make a good lawyer. I thought that sounded like a good job and for at least a year that became my goal in life. However, one day our basketball coach, whom I admired very much, asked each member of the class to stand and tell what they would like to be when they grew up. When my turn came I announced that I would like to be a lawyer. My teacher immediately responded: "That's foolish! Lawyers are a dime a dozen."

This made such an impression on me I abandoned the law before I had even started.

After a short stint in the Navy, I returned to the University of Iowa and received my B.A. degree. I tried becoming a sports announcer, a teacher and, then a Boy Scouts Executive. I accepted the Boy Scouts job, but I needed a car. I wrote to an uncle in Chicago, who was a very successful lawyer, to see if he would lend me $500 to buy a Kaiser Frasier automobile. He wrote back with the best advice I have ever received. "Scouting is a great avocation, but I don't think it is a very good vocation. You have always liked debate and politics—have you ever thought about becoming a lawyer?" Shades of seventh grade. I took the advice and went to law school and I have never regretted it.

I graduated from the University of Iowa Law School in February of 1951. Dean Ladd wanted me to go to a firm where I could get trial experience and I was fortunate to be hired at the prestigious Omaha law firm of Kennedy, Holland, Delacy and Svoboda. I worked directly with the dean of Nebraska trial lawyers, George "Skip" Delacy. I had been in the firm for only a few months when upon arriving at work one day he told me he wanted me to defend a suit against the Omaha Street

Railway Company. Wow! I bubbled over with excitement which, however, was short lived. The head claims adjustor for the company virtually exploded when informed of Delacy's decision. "Delacy, it is not your money that is at risk," he shouted. "I won't allow you to send in this kid alone." For the next few minutes the two of them argued; finally the adjustor agreed to let me "first chair" the trial, but only if Delacy closely supervised. We proceeded to the courthouse where the bailiff called 18 persons as prospective jurors into the jury box. Just then Delacy rose, gave a note to the court reporter and left the room. The reporter gave it to me. It said: "Good Luck, Don, it is all yours." My stomach churned. Fortunately, I won the case. If I had lost I doubt I would have tried another case again.

After four years, I received an attractive offer to go with a larger firm in Milwaukee, trying insurance defense cases. I did this for almost two years and then the senior partner I worked for was appointed to the federal bench. I returned to Omaha, and soon Leo Eisenstatt and I started our own firm. We practiced together in a small group until President Johnson appointed me to the Circuit Court of Appeal in 1966. I went directly from the trial practice to the appeals court. However, I have always felt the true romance of the law was in the trial courtroom, and have frequently volunteered to sit as a district trial judge trying cases. I relate this background primarily to give an overview of my experience.

Notwithstanding society's current love affair with "lawyer-bashing," my life as a lawyer and judge has provided a firm conviction that the legal profession in the United States is the greatest profession in the world. It is a proud profession and deservedly so, for without it, the Bill of Rights would have no vitality. Government without opposition would decide, through those in power, what is best for all of us. Without dedicated advocates to urge the rights of divided interests, we would not have public and private accountability, we would not have adequate respect for the privacy of the individual, and we would not pay sufficient heed to the vested rights of individuals as well as private and public entrepreneurs.

This book is written for the advocate who wishes to dedicate his or her career to maintaining our quality of life and making it better than it is. It is about advocacy—about the roles played by lawyers, judges, witnesses, and juries in the litigation process. Contrary to popular belief, law is hardly a science where degrees of certainty exist. The litigation process involves the law, but the decisional outcomes rest, more often than not, on the interactions of the people involved.

PROLOGUE

It is my hope that what is written here can serve to help the lawyer, young and old, to improve the legal process. My purpose is not to provide mechanical guidance on how to cross-examine, how to offer exhibits into evidence, and other aspects of trial practice, as many books do. I share the observations of many seasoned lawyers who have concluded that the diverse interrelated roles that people serve in the trial process more often dictate end results in litigation than does the law itself. Without basic behavioral instincts to guide us, all the mechanical rules and procedures are of little importance. Thus, my purpose in writing these chapters is to use empirical anecdotes to alert the aspiring student as well as the seasoned lawyer to the basic human goals essential for success in litigation. In addition, I hope non-law trained people will find these few chapters interesting reading and instructive about the adversarial process by which, we, the people, seek to obtain justice in our legal system.

The reader should understand that the role of the lawyer is not always easy. This is particularly true for those who engage in litigation. There can be great stress and disappointment. But it must be balanced against the ongoing satisfaction in helping others. Frustration will override if the lawyer's goal is material gain; satisfaction will be dominant if the lawyer's goal is dedication to others. That is what the profession is all about.

In a play by an English playwright a fictitious character, J. F. Shade, related the differences in classical and romantic literature, and observed that "we balance reason against imagination, logic against emotion, geometry against nature, formality against spontaneity, discretion against valour . . . but in so doing, we are drawing attention not so much to different aesthetic principles as to different responses to the world, to different tempers." Although not his intent in writing this passage, the playwright has established the contrast between what law is popularly thought to be (logic, reason, formality, etc.) and what trial advocacy actually is ("different responses . . . . to different tempers.")

A law suit necessarily involves legal rules developed by logic and reasoning, but the litigation process is much more. Trial advocacy involves human psychology more than it does rules of law. My goal in writing of trial experiences is not simply to tell "war stories." Every trial lawyer has a closet full of those. And to a great extent, this book reveals many of mine gathered from close to a half a century as a trial lawyer and judge. I describe these incidents to help young lawyers be aware of the human processes that are involved in striving to achieve a fairer system of justice.

PROLOGUE

One of the problems in law school is that we teach legal theory and legal methods without the recognition that the practice of law is not really about "law." Rather, it is about "life." I have always thought that after the mind is disciplined to legal thinking in the first year of law school, the law curriculum should require each student to participate in graduate study of liberal arts for three hours each semester. The students should study human psychology, literature, physics, mathematics, social sciences, chemistry, English composition, and history. Each of these courses provides a disciplined study in human behavior and human nature missing from the pure legal curriculum. To me, this is more important than the debate over whether law schools should adopt more clinical training. Lawyers should receive greater training to solve life's problems. Perhaps this is what Justice Holmes had in mind when he wrote "The life of the law is not logic, it is experience."

Dean Mason Ladd was and still is well-known for his contribution to the field of evidence. In the eyes of many, and certainly in mine, he was the Wigmore and Morgan of our day. He always told me that to be a good trial lawyer "you have to have it in your genes." I think to a great extent this is true. Mason Ladd made the law of evidence interesting because he used illustrations and stories to make the rules and principles come alive. He provided a human personality to technical application of legal jargon. He was a gifted teacher, a master at story telling to help us remember important rules. I hope, in this little book, that I can do the same.

I wish to thank several people who have encouraged me to write this book. Many lawyers and judges have offered friendly editorial advice. I want to particularly thank two of my former law clerks who have volunteered their time to help me present these ideas in a readable way. They were Carolyn Brue and Dan Oberdorfer. I also want to thank Judy Anderson, who has spent extra hours at home in typing my rough, rough drafts. I wish particularly to thank Jack Higgins, my former partner, Len Keyes, a former judge and great lawyer, Professor Bob Oliphant and Professor Neil Hamilton at William Mitchell College of Law for their helpful suggestions. Of course, I want to thank my wife, Miriam, for her support not only in this endeavor but in everything I have attempted. She and my five wonderful daughters have given me the encouragement and love to keep all things going and under control.

CHAPTER I
THE LAWYER

INTRODUCTION

INTENSITY

Always Be Willing To Walk The Extra Mile For Your Client

A Lack Of Preparation Can Cause Immense Damage

A SENSE OF FAIR PLAY

*Always Be Open And Above Board In Your Dealings
With The Court And Opposing Counsel*

Do Not Ever Try To Hide The Truth

RESOURCEFULNESS

The Art Of Persuasion Lies In The Skill Of Corroboration

Reproducing The Accident Scene

A Witness Does Not Belong To Either Side

Exhibit One—The Adverse Witness

SINCERITY

The Client's Story Must Be Believable

Preparation Makes An Advocate More Believable

COMMON SENSE

*Counsel Cannot Make Strategic Choices At Trial Without A
Thorough Knowledge Of The Law And The Facts*

*Counsel Must Use Common Sense
To Anticipate Where A Trial Is Heading*

INTRODUCTION

One of America's greatest federal trial judges was my friend, the Honorable James McMillan of Charlotte, North Carolina. He was an outstanding trial lawyer before he went on to the bench. His most outstanding attribute was that he understood people and had great compassion for everyone, rich or poor, white or black, old or young. It made no difference to him. He once observed: "I sometimes tell lawyers, there may be more foundation for a successful law practice in the Sermon on the Mount than in the law books." This is perhaps the best advice that could be given to any lawyer.

From my experience at the bar and bench, I would suggest there are five basic characteristics that lawyers, either in trial or in appellate advocacy, should possess to attain success: (1) intensity, (2) a sense of fair play, (3) resourcefulness, (4) sincerity, and (5) common sense.

INTENSITY

Intensity can be defined in different ways, but in the litigation process it boils down to the idea that the work of counsel never ends. The skilled advocate must never quit probing, searching, and exploring for ideas and evidence to carry the burden of winning the client's case.

The annals of American jurisprudence carry names of lawyers who have served as outstanding advocates. Men such as Daniel Webster and Clarence Darrow have long incited the spirit of the would-be advocate in and out of the courtroom. Yet, the bare truth, as both Webster and Darrow admitted in their writings, is that the true genius of the skilled advocate is in the intensity of preparation. Diligence and industry before and during trial have won many lawsuits.

Always Be Willing To Walk
The Extra Mile For Your Client

As a trial attorney, I encountered some lawyers who rarely bothered to interview witnesses before they placed them on the stand. I thought this was just pure laziness. It is helpful to interview every witness who is available, whether hostile or not, at least once or twice before trial.

I recall a lawsuit over a tragic, double fatality traffic accident in which an interview with a hostile witness made the difference between winning and losing the case. I represented the estates of the two decedents. They were mother and father to three surviving infants. An oil tanker truck had turned in front of the decedents' vehicle at a Y-intersection. The witness had observed the collision. We obtained his statement through pretrial exchange of information established by rules of procedure. The witness's statement related that the decedents were traveling at a speed of 80 miles per hour just before the collision. *One thing you learn in the world of litigation is that statements given by lay witnesses more often reflect the interest of the person taking the statement than they do the witness's actual observations.* This is particularly true for opinions on factors such as speed and distance. Oddly enough, the witness was a court reporter in Toledo, Ohio. He had been written up in Ripley's *Believe It Or Not* as the fastest one-fingered typist in the world. Shortly before trial, the oil company scheduled a deposition for the witness on a Monday morning in Toledo.

I was very suspicious of the statement because it was hand written by an adjuster for the company that had insured the oil rig. It was obvious to me that the oil company's attorney, a well-known lawyer in Toledo, knew the court reporter. The two had worked in the same legal circles for many years. Testimony from an independent witness that our vehicle was traveling 80 miles an hour could be extremely damaging. Such speed would have been clearly in excess of the posted limit and would have been evidence of negligence on the part of the decedent driver. It might have been sufficient to bar recovery as a matter of law, or at least prejudice the plaintiff's case in the eyes of the jury.

I decided to leave early for Toledo and try to interview the witness before the scheduled deposition. After arriving in Toledo early Sunday afternoon, I telephoned the witness's home but no one answered. The phone book listed five other individuals with the same last name. I began to call each one to see if they could help find the witness. On the third call, I located the witness's brother. He told me that the witness and his wife were at their lake cabin, one hundred miles from Toledo. They were closing down the cabin that day and were planning to return to Toledo late that evening. He gave me the telephone number.

I reached the witness about 4:00 that afternoon. He said he would not return to Toledo until the next morning. The deposition was scheduled at 9:00 a.m., and he planned to drive from the lake to his home early enough in the morning to be there on time. I told him how

4

important it was that I visit with him before the deposition. Unfortunately, that evening he and his wife were having a big get-together with their friends and neighbors on the lake because this was the last day of the summer and everybody was going home. He was very friendly and told me I was welcome to come to their party.

I decided to do just that. I rented a car. It took me almost three hours to find the lake cottage tucked back on winding country roads, but I finally arrived. In the front yard were at least a hundred people enjoying the weather, a cook out, and two kegs of beer. The witness told me to partake and introduce myself to their friends, which I did. This was no time to attempt to visit with him about the matters at hand. At about midnight everyone began to go home, and at 1:00 a.m., I was alone with the witness and his wife.

I showed him the statement that the adjuster had taken and told him how important it was to my clients (the surviving children) that the accurate facts be disclosed. He told me, as I had surmised, that the insurance adjuster had suggested the speed of 80 miles an hour. He said that the car had passed him on the highway about a mile and a half from the scene of the accident. He was going about 50 miles an hour and all he could really say is that the passing vehicle was going faster than he was. He stated he could not pinpoint the car's actual speed at the time of the accident.

I visited with these nice people late into the night. I arrived back at the hotel at about 5:30 in the morning, arose at about 8:00, had breakfast and went to the opposing lawyer's office. I was sitting in the waiting room when the witness and his wife arrived exactly at 9:00 a.m.

The attorney introduced me to the witness and I indicated that I was pleased to see him again. The lawyer then said: "I'd like a few minutes alone with the witness before we take the deposition." I acknowledged that that was his prerogative. They were in conference for about fifteen minutes before opposing counsel called me for the beginning of the deposition. The deposition proceeded with the attorney asking about what had happened. As far as I was concerned the only reason for the deposition was to establish the speed of the decedents' vehicle. Much to my surprise, the direct examination ended with no questions about this crucial point. I stated I had no questions on cross-examination and the witness left.

Later the attorney told me that he couldn't understand what had happened. He said the witness had given a written statement about the speed of the vehicle, but during his interview with him before the deposition, the witness said that he was not in a position to give an opinion on speed. I could never understand why the attorney did not ask the witness how fast he was going to at least lay the inference that the deceased parents were driving faster than 50 miles an hour. He didn't bother even to do that. I am confident that without the interview the night before, opposing counsel could have easily induced the witness to testify in accord with the insurance adjuster's statement of excessive speed. The extra effort in questioning the witness's statement *before* the deposition made the difference between winning and losing the case.

A Lack Of Preparation Can Cause Immense Damage

One of my cases was called to trial unexpectedly. The bailiff telephoned informing me that the prior case had settled and the judge wanted the lawyers in my case to come over at 2:00 p.m. to pick a jury. The judge planned on having opening statements that afternoon and to start the evidence the next morning. My client was the insurance company. The insured was the defendant. I called him and asked him to take off work so he could be present when I chose the jury. *You never want to give the impression that your client isn't interested in who will be chosen to sit on the jury.*

The dispute was whether the plaintiff had driven into a bad snow storm in the mountains without putting chains on his car. He ultimately got stuck on a steep hill and my client collided with him. The plaintiff was not present in the courtroom that afternoon. Counsel explained that his client would appear the next day after the jury was chosen and opening statements were made. In his opening statement, plaintiff's counsel told the jury that the storm came up unexpectedly *after his client had left home* and that he did not have time to put on his chains. In my opening statement, I said that our evidence would show that the plaintiff was contributorily negligent for leaving home in the middle of the storm without chains.

When the plaintiff testified in his case in chief, he gave a third version of what had happened. He testified that he had put on his chains before he left home but the ice on the mountain hill was so slick he could not control his car. On cross-examination I confronted the plaintiff with what his lawyer had said in his opening statement. He said his lawyer was wrong. In closing argument, I challenged the plaintiff's credibility by using his lawyer's explanation given during his opening statement as a direct contradiction for the jury to weigh.

Plaintiff's counsel argued that the jury should disregard his opening statement because he was mistaken. The jurors rejected the plaintiff's story. They told me later that they thought that in his opening statement the lawyer had accurately reported what his client told him, and that his client lied from the witness stand. Thus, the jury believed the lawyer and not his client. I am convinced his client told the truth and his lawyer lost the case.

The basic lesson to be learned is that every lawyer owes an ethical duty to his client to prepare the case continually. You must do whatever you can to present your case in the best light. At the same time, no lawyer should to do anything unethical. Lawyers should never attempt to suborn perjury or to produce false evidence.

A SENSE OF FAIR PLAY

In his book "Confronting Injustice," Edmond Cahn wrote that justice is best defined by describing injustice. Similarly, appropriate courtroom tactics perhaps can be gauged best by examples of improper behavior.

Always Be Open And Above Board In Your Dealings With The Court And Opposing Counsel

Many plaintiff's lawyers refuse to handle railroad crossing accident cases because they are difficult to win in the absence of proof of a dangerous crossing. In many states, automobile drivers are required to stop at every railroad crossing. The unusual fact of one case we handled was that two members of the railroad crew saw the automobile stop before crossing the tracks. We used this testimony to our advantage when representing the decedent's estate.

We contended at trial that the train, without headlights, crashed into our client's vehicle while the railroad was switching cars just after dusk. The railroad crew explained that the engineer could see the signals from the brakemen better without the glare of the engine's headlights because it was dusk. The railroad argued that upon proper lookout, the driver should have seen the approaching engine illuminated against the remaining light in the sky. We claimed it was too dark to see the engine approaching without a headlight.

To prove that the engine could have been seen silhouetted against the sky, the railroad requested that a state highway patrol officer, whom we had previously called as a witness for the plaintiff, go to the scene of the accident to take photographs of an approaching switch engine. The trial was approximately one year from the date of the collision. The pictures were taken at five minute intervals. I arrived at the courtroom early the morning after the patrol officer visited the scene. Arriving early is a good practice for all trial counsel to follow. While organizing my material and notes, I noticed the two railroad lawyers looking at a series of photographs which I later learned had been taken by the patrolman the night before. The senior trial counsel for the railroad told his junior partner, "No, no—don't use those two—they are too dark." There is nothing unethical in listening and observing opposing counsel in plain view.

When the trial proceeded, the railroad's counsel called the highway patrolman and marked four photographs as exhibits. I could have questioned whether the photos were substantially similar to what plaintiff saw one year ago. Rather than raise a foundation objection, I asked to view the photos, which showed the engine, without head-lights, clearly silhouetted and visible against a gray sky in the background. I stated I did not wish to make any objection as long as *all* photographs taken were produced. The trial judge turned to the railroad counsel and in the presence of the jury inquired: "Are these all of the pictures?" Lead counsel for the railroad turned to his assistant and said: "Well, I think these are all the photos we have. Do we have any other photos?" I interrupted, "When I arrived this morning I thought I saw a couple more photos which you put back in the briefcase." Lead railroad counsel said, "We'll certainly check—my investigator was in charge of the photos." The briefcase was opened and, lo and behold, two more photos were discovered! Both were endorsed on the back as having been taken within five minutes of the time when the accident occurred. They were black as night—no train was silhouetted. The combined deceit of the lawyers backfired. Within those few seconds, a difficult case was won. The railroad would have been better off to have left all of the exhibits at the office.

Do Not Ever Try To Hide The Truth

A few years ago, I was sitting as a trial judge in a case brought by an airline passenger who claimed he suffered a back injury when the plane flew into severe turbulence. A local physician opined that the plaintiff would require surgery. Under pretrial rules and the court's pretrial order, the parties were to exchange all medical reports. On cross-examination, the airline's lawyer asked the physician if he had sought a second opinion about the plaintiff's condition. The doctor answered that he had not. However, he volunteered that the plaintiff told him that his attorney had referred him to a well-known neurologist for an evaluation. Counsel for the airline asked for a recess. In chambers, defense counsel stated that the plaintiff had not produced a medical report from the consulting specialist. Plaintiff's counsel responded he had no memory of any referral and that he had searched his file and had not found a report. I told counsel that I would recess the trial until the next day. I asked counsel for the plaintiff to inquire of the neurologist, make the neurologist available to defense counsel for interviews and, if necessary, for deposition.

The next morning plaintiff's counsel arrived early and requested an in-chambers conference. He apologetically explained he did not turn the report over because his secretary had misplaced it in his correspondence file. I viewed the explanation with great skepticism. The report revealed the specialist's findings to be entirely negative. As a witness for the defense, the neurologist testified plaintiff had not suffered an injury of consequence. The jury rejected plaintiff's claim of severe injury despite strong evidence of negligence on the part of the airline.

Sometimes in the zeal to win their case certain lawyers justify cutting corners and do not play fair with their adversaries. In my experience as counsel and judge, this always reflects negatively, as it should, on the client's case. Every trial lawyer must strive for integrity and maintain the respect of his peers as well as the judiciary.

RESOURCEFULNESS

In every phase of a case, investigation, pleading, discovery, etc., trial counsel should be continually alert as to how he or she may best persuade the judge and the jury that their client's claim can be vindicated. The more a lawyer can be resourceful in drawing upon his or her creativity and originality, the better chance of catching opposing counsel off guard, but more importantly providing an interesting, persuasive basis to your proof. The more you can utilize your resourcefulness to corroborate your client's version of the case, the more successful you will become.

CHAPTER I — THE LAWYER

The Art Of Persuasion Lies In The Skill Of Corroboration

We had a case years ago where our client severely injured his back while working as a lineman for a major railroad. His job was to replace telegraph poles that had blown down along the track. He did this by taking new poles off a side car and manually hoisting them into the hole. This was arduous work. Before hurting his back, our client had complained to the railroad that it was too much for one man to do.

Our lawsuit claimed that the railroad had not provided a safe place for the employee to work. The railroad responded that the plaintiff had failed to follow the proper procedures for replacing telegraph poles. As we did in every case, we submitted interrogatories asking the railroad whether it had photographs or motion pictures relating to the accident. The railroad responded that it had made a motion picture of the proper manner to unload and place poles in the ground without risk of injury.

We requested production of the film. The video film showed an individual single-handedly removing a pole from the sidecar and placing it in the ground. I noticed that even on the film this appeared to be arduous work, and so I asked to depose the lineman shown on the movie. He was a supervisor who worked in a different locale. During the course of his deposition, I showed the film. He testified it depicted the proper way to place a pole in the ground, but when I asked him if this is the way that he placed poles in the ground when he actually performed his job, he said: "No."

I asked him to describe how he did the work. He said: "Well, I have a truck and a hoist. I would never put a pole in the ground manually because lifting the pole is too heavy and could hurt my back."

I did not make a big thing of this until trial. At the outset of trial, I subpoenaed the supervisor, showed the video, and asked the supervisor the same question I had propounded in the deposition. He testified, as he had in the deposition, that he did not place poles in the ground manually, but that the railroad furnished him a truck and a hoist to do the work. We had won the case through the use of the railroad's own witness.

RESOURCEFULNESS

Reproducing The Accident Scene

One of the last cases I tried as a lawyer involved a plane crash in Denver, Colorado, that killed both the pilot and the co-pilot. My client was a widow who represented the estate of her deceased husband. The decedent owned a local air commuter service in Nebraska, and when he died, he was on a personal business trip to the West Coast. Because he had never flown over mountains, he had hired a co-pilot from another air taxi service to help. The two pilots left Columbus, Nebraska in a Twin Beach aircraft with dual controls. When they were in the process of landing at an airport near Denver, they collided with a Piper aircraft that was doing touch-and-go landings. The FAA investigation concluded that the pilot of the Nebraska plane had misjudged the location of the Piper aircraft and was at fault. My client's body was found in the right hand seat of the wreckage, and the air taxi pilot, who was also killed in the crash, was found in the left hand seat.

The question was: Who was flying the plane? With dual controls either of the two pilots was capable of flying the Twin Beach. The defense argued that the purpose of hiring an air taxi pilot was to help fly over the mountains. Because they had not reached the mountains, the defense urged that my client was flying his own plane. I retained an experienced pilot to testify as an expert witness. He opined the air taxi pilot in the left hand seat was flying the plane because the final approach pattern that day required the plane to make two 90-degree left turns. This was not a radio controlled landing and only the left-seat pilot had full observation of the field below at all times.

Of course, expert testimony is simply opinion evidence and does not constitute direct evidence. It can easily be believed or disbelieved depending upon the demeanor and credibility of the witness. Our expert told me I could better understand his testimony if I went up with him in a dual controlled plane. We made two approaches. In one instance he sat in the right hand seat and I sat in the left. I was not a pilot, but I could see the clearance of the field from the left side. On the right hand side, I had limited visibility. I decided the best way to demonstrate this was to take a photographer up in the plane and have him take a motion picture of the two landings —one sitting from the left seat and the other from the right seat. His movie allowed the jury to observe and corroborate what the expert was saying. Corroboration of a witness's important testimony can be a persuasive evidentiary tool. Because the jury believed our expert and the documentation of his evidence, we won the case.

A Witness Does Not Belong To Either Side

Resourcefulness requires a recognition that all witnesses may be used by either side. During the course of a trial an attorney has to be constantly alert for evidence that he or she has not anticipated. This may occur even when attorneys exchange witness lists. A few years ago, we represented a local steel company employee whose job was to help unload steel beams from a gondola railroad car using a hoist and chains. The beams weighed in excess of 4,000 pounds each. One day an adjacent stack of beams toppled and crushed our client's leg. After the accident, another employee noticed a short beam on the bottom of the stack and surmised the beams had not been properly stacked when originally loaded at a U.S. Steel Plant near Chicago. We sued U.S. Steel claiming negligence. U.S. Steel in turn sued the railroad that had delivered the car.

In his opening statement before the jury, U.S. Steel's lawyer indicated that he was going to call the owner of the local steel company as a witness. He said the owner would testify how his own employees were negligent by remaining within the gondola car when the beams were being unloaded. The defense lawyer's theory was that once the employees strapped the chains to the beams, they should get out of the way before the beams were hoisted from the car. This made a lot of sense and was probably correct. However, there were no printed rules to that effect. According to other employees, everyone unloaded the cars in the same way our client did. The foreman of the plant knew this and had never objected to the manner in which the beams were unloaded.

I was worried that the local owner would go out of his way to assist U.S. Steel in his testimony. He was a good friend of the defense lawyer. His company did a lot of business with U.S. Steel. I presumed he did not think much of the fact that his employee was suing his customer. Knowing time was short, I called the owner at his plant. He stated that he was just going to lunch before coming to court at 1:30 p.m. I asked him if he would wait for ten minutes because I wanted to show him something very important relating to the trial. When I arrived, I told him I was quite sure that we could obtain a favorable judgment against U.S. Steel. If we did, U.S. Steel had already filed a third party lawsuit seeking indemnification from the railroad. I informed him that because of his company's indemnity agreement with the railroad, if there was any evidence of negligence by the local steel company, his company could end up paying the entire judgment. I reminded him that his plant foreman was present at the unloading and did not object to the manner in which my client unloaded the gondola car. I also told him he must tell the truth from the witness stand, but that I was going to question him about his company's custom and practice in unloading the beams. It seemed to me, as I told the owner, that it was certainly debatable whether my client was negligent if he was merely following company practice. I suggested he discuss the situation with his company's lawyer.

When we returned to the court, the defense lawyer announced that he had called the local steel company and the owner was still out to lunch. He elected to go forward with other evidence. He had not subpoenaed the owner. He put in his evidence in half a day and at 4:00 p.m. he once again called the owner of the company. He learned the owner still had not come back from lunch. For whatever reason, the owner chose not to testify.

The client recovered a sizeable judgment. There is no question that his case would have been harmed if the owner of the company had testified that my client was negligent. Did I behave ethically or should I have been subject to criticism for discussing the case with the owner? There is nothing improper with exploring all of the facts in a case with any possible unrepresented witness.

Exhibit One—The Adverse Witness

One time I represented a building contractor. He hired only non-union help. The union picketed his work at a building site. The contractor one day became disturbed and went over to one of the picketers and tore off the sign he was carrying which was protesting the use of non-union labor. Shortly thereafter, the business agent for the union appeared at the scene. He brought along approximately ten thugs, which I later appropriately described as the "goon" squad. The business agent confronted the contractor and suddenly hit him on the side of the face with some brass knuckles. It caused a terrible injury resulting in the fracture of all of the jaw and facial bones and left some residual brain damage. The contractor went out of control, enraged, he picked up an axe and blindly chased the business agent. If he had not been stopped by some of his own workmen, he would have killed the agent. While this was gong on, the thugs began to chase some of the work crew. One of the thugs was known as "Jake." He was about six foot eight and had a muscular frame. He picked up a two by four and started to chase some of the workmen.

We sued the local union, an incorporated association, the international union, and each of the officers of the union. The trial was a great cause celebré. It lasted six weeks. I had earlier taken the depositions of as many of the thugs as we could identify, including Jake. He appeared at the deposition half drunk. He had heavy facial scarring. In appearance, he came close to resembling Boris Karloff made up as Frankenstein. I made up my mind, regardless of his testimony, I wanted him to be Exhibit One at trial. Jake had moved from his old address since his deposition however, and we could not find him. I issued a subpoena for him at the Union Hall. The deputy sheriff reported that no one knew him. I sent out an investigator. He tracked Jake down to a tavern near the Union Hall. It appeared that Jake always showed up at the tavern at 7:30 every morning. The investigator said that Jake started his day off with two shots of whiskey every morning. Although Jake had denied in his deposition as being nothing more than a passive eye witness on the day of the assault, I wanted the jury to get a good look at him. I requested the sheriff go to the tavern at 7:30 the next morning to serve Jake the subpoena.

Around ten that morning we were putting on some of our testimony. On the other side of the counsel table was the union's array of lawyers. I saw the young assistant leave the room and then immediately came back and whispered to the counsel in front of him, who in turn, told the second lawyer who then whispered audibly to the lead attorney "Jake is out in the hall." Lead counsel turned and said, "Tell him to get the hell out of here." The word was passed down to the assistant and the assistant responded back through the chain of attorneys, and I again overheard the second lawyer whisper to lead counsel, "He's got a subpoena." I then called Jake as a witness. He lumbered in. I'll never forget his appearance. His eyes were bloodshot, his hair uncombed, and he had a tatoo on his right arm. I asked him about his activities on the day in question. He once again denied any role in the incident other than admitting that he was at the scene. I then asked, if, in fact, didn't he chase some of the work crew with a two by four. I still have the visual recall of him clinching his fists and shouting, "Are you calling me a liar?" I told him, "No, I am just trying to get you to tell the truth." Our next witness was one of the work crew who then identified Jake as the man who had chased him that morning with a two by four.

As I stated, even though he was a potential witness for the union (and one they would never call), Jake was our best witness at the trial. When the verdict was returned, it was the largest verdict in the history of the state, although it has been surpassed many times since.

SINCERITY

All lawyers, by their demeanor and actions, must display confidence in their case. Lawyers are unlikely to be sincere when they present a concocted, illogical theory of their case. The lawyer who is not well prepared cannot show sincerity. The lawyer must work with the client to create an effective, sincere presentation. The lawyer's confidence is directly tied to demonstrable sincerity.

The Client's Story Must Be Believable

Several years ago another lawyer asked me to represent his client in a boiler explosion case. The lawyer thought he could settle the case without trial, but had been unsuccessful in doing so. When he approached me, the case had already been placed on the trial calendar. I agreed to try the case only if I could get a 30 day postponement to prepare. The court reluctantly granted me the needed time.

The client owned a large warehouse. He had leased the bottom and top floors to two corporations that stored merchandise. He claimed he was not responsible for the explosion because the boilers were in good repair and had overheated when the thermostat failed to function properly. The plaintiffs demanded a total of $500,000 for their lost merchandise. One of the plaintiffs was a toy wholesaler and had thousands of small toys in inventory for sale at Christmas. My investigation demonstrated to me that our client, who had no liability insurance, was not credible. He had repaired the boilers himself and had patched rusted breaks in the boiler pipes with rubber inner-tubes. I discovered that the thermostat had broken down on several prior occasions and the client had personally attempted to repair it. I told the client that if he were to take the stand and testify as he did in his earlier deposition (given before I entered the case), the jury would not believe him and would punish him with a large damage award against him. I demonstrated to him how the fire marshal's investigation would impeach his testimony. I recommended we admit liability for the boiler explosion. After all, it was his building and his boiler that blew up. I told him I would tell the jury the only reason we were in trial was because the two corporations who leased space were attempting to obtain excessive damages. He agreed with this approach. The court allowed me to reopen discovery to take several depositions challenging the plaintiffs' proof of damage. Their inventory papers were highly questionable. After opening statement, the plaintiff corporations were on the defensive, not the owner of the building. We settled the case for $75,000 after the first day of trial. It was a very fair settlement for our client.

Preparation Makes An Advocate More Believable

Courtroom rules do not allow lawyers to vouch for the truthfulness of their case. This is because a lawyer is not a witness and cannot testify. Even though overt vouching is prohibited and can constitute prejudicial error, in actuality the credibility of the lawyer is the key to successful persuasion.

Lawyers who must move on to a different line of questioning because they are unable to find an exhibit after fumbling around in stacks of papers lose the orderly sequence of proof and no small measure of believability. This is not resurrected when, after lunch, the lawyer says to the judge—"I found the exhibit I was looking for this morning and now wish to offer it into evidence." It can be relevant and admissible, but the significance of the evidence may be lost to the jury outside the context of the morning's evidence.

Effective impeachment of a witness from a prior sworn deposition or statement also requires preparation and organization as the following two examples show. First, the ill prepared examination:

> Q: Isn't it true that when you gave your deposition you stated you did not have a meeting with X?
>
> A: I don't remember.
>
> Q: Well, let me ask you if you didn't make the following answer in your deposition? Pause—pause—(counsel paging through deposition)—pause—pause—"Well, I can't find it right now, but let me ask you this (changing to a different question).

In the above example, counsel lost credibility with the jury and probably with the court. How much more effective if counsel might say:

Q: You say you had a meeting with X and discussed the terms of the contract.

A: Yes.

Q: Do you remember when I took your deposition?

A: Yes.

Q: At that time, on page 28, line 10, didn't I ask you the following question and did you not make the following answer: Question: Did you ever have a meeting with X to negotiate the contract? Answer: I never met with X to discuss the terms of the contract.

Effective cross-examination depends on counsel outlining the deposition by line and page. In the first instance, the jury may suspect counsel is bluffing; in the second, the jury is assured counsel knows the case.

COMMON SENSE

Every trial lawyer should use common sense. Good judgment can often affect the result of litigation. Many lawyers feel the question of judgment is so highly subjective that predicting good judgment is too amorphous to be worthy of concern. I disagree. I believe good judgment can be developed by thorough study, preparation, and organization.

Counsel Cannot Make Strategic Choices At Trial Without A Thorough Knowledge Of The Law And The Facts

I once presided over a case in which the defendant was trying to avoid liability for consequential damages from an alleged breach of contract. The lawyer representing the plaintiff had written a letter *rescinding* the contract at the time of the alleged breach. In his complaint, the lawyer for the plaintiff asked for alternative remedies: (1) rescission of the contract or (2) damages for breach of contract. Under rescission, plaintiff would be entitled only to the return of his initial payment and incidental expenses. Under a breach of contract, the defendant could be liable for all foreseeable damages flowing from the breach—so-called consequential damages. In this case, the consequential damages were potentially very large. They included the loss of the business, lost profits, lost good will and other intangible damages.

While presiding over the pretrial conference, I asked plaintiff's counsel whether he intended to elect his remedy, rescission or breach of contract. He stated, almost with belligerent erudition, that the law allowed him to proceed alternatively, and that he did not have to make an election. This was true. As I told him, however, I would instruct the jury that if it found rescission, the plaintiff could not collect for consequential damages. The exercise of good judgment at this point would have been to dismiss the claim for rescission and to proceed solely under the breach of contract theory.

Notwithstanding these facts, plaintiff steadfastly chose not to elect his remedies. The trial began. On the cross-examination of the plaintiff, the defendant offered into evidence the letter written by plaintiff's counsel, on behalf of the plaintiff, rescinding the contract. For the first time, plaintiff's counsel realized his claim for rescission, if successful, would bar his client from collecting any consequential damage. Plaintiff's counsel, upon the offer of his letter, stood and loudly stated: "I object." I asked: "On what grounds?" He sputtered: "Attorney-client privilege and hearsay." The objection was absurd. I overruled the objection. The end result was inevitable. The jury found that plaintiff had rescinded the contract and no consequential damages were awarded. I believe proper preparation would have made a difference. Of course, counsel's lack of knowledge of the rules of evidence didn't help the matter, but his error merely compounded his early irrational and fatal decision.

Counsel Must Use Common Sense
To Anticipate Where A Trial Is Heading

Poor judgment can be manifested in many ways. I once tried a simple rear-end collision case in which my client's vehicle was hit from behind while stopped at a red light. The driver of the other car was intoxicated even though the accident occurred at noon. Before checking on the condition of the injured driver, he ran across the street to a bar for more liquor. When the police arrived, he was at the scene drinking a bottle of beer. The only issue that needed to be tried was the extent of my client's injury. She had a bad neck sprain; in those days the doctors called it "whiplash." We offered to settle for $5,000. We thought this offer was high but we were willing to negotiate.

The defendant filed an answer to our complaint which generally denied every allegation. At trial, the pleadings had not been amended, and we decided that in the opening statement, as early as possible, state to the jury that "the defendant was drunk at high noon." The defendant's counsel in opening statement stated that the only issue was that of damage. We proceeded with the proof of our case. I called the police officer who arrived at the scene, who had observed the defendant drinking from his newly purchased bottle of beer. As I began to inquire of the officer, defendant's counsel requested a bench conference. He stated to the judge, on the record, that he wished to stipulate to liability and therefore any reference to defendant's intoxication was irrelevant. The court so ordered. When I tried to ask the officer what he had observed, the defendant objected. The court sustained the objection and told the jury that the defendant had stipulated to liability.

At recess, the defendant's counsel, as relayed to me later, approached the judge's law clerk and stated, "We really pulled a coup by stipulating to our liability. We prevented them from presenting all the evidence about drinking." Where was counsel when the lights were turned on? Obviously, defendant should have admitted liability in his pleading. The wisdom of stipulation came too late. The jury went to the jury room knowing the defendant was "drunk at high noon." The verdict was $15,000. The verdict has always reminded me that juries do not necessarily compensate plaintiffs; they punish defendants. If the defendant had collided with the plaintiff because his brakes failed or because of an icy road, the verdict would have been much less. Counsel failed to exercise common sense.

CHAPTER II
THE CLIENT

RELATIONSHIP OF THE LAWYER TO THE CLIENT
"Baby, I Love You. I Will Always Be There When You Need Me."

The Client's Best Interest

Consulting With The Client

The Client's Role On Strategic Decisions

Overstating The Likelihood Of Success To The Client

Understating The Value Of The Case To The Client

The Client Discharges The Lawyer

Investigate The Client's Case Before You File Suit

PLEADING AND THE CLIENT
Consulting With Your Client As To What You Plead

The Difficult Client

The Egg Case

Whatever The Cost, The Attorney-Client Privilege Must Be Honored

THE ATTORNEY FEE
To Fee Or Not To Fee

Charging No Fee

Charging A Reduced Fee

Referral Cases

Don't Be Greedy

Whatever Happens, Be Ethical

RELATIONSHIP OF THE LAWYER TO THE CLIENT

"Baby, I Love You. I Will Always
Be There When You Need Me."

The above is a current lyric to a popular song. It may sound trite, but all lawyers should establish their relationship with their client with such an attitude. Unfortunately, too many lawyers look upon their clientele with the opposite feelings. Many lawyers do not want to be bothered by their client. I know lawyers who never return their clients' phone calls. They have too much to do or perhaps they find the client a bore. Many lawyers, once they have been retained, find their clients to be interlopers in the case. The fundamental error many lawyers make is that they feel that it is *their* lawsuit that is being tried. These type of lawyers seldom keep their clients informed of the progress of the litigation. Lawyers know that most of their clients do not understand the law or what is going on and, therefore, their attitude is why take the time to consult with them.

Many lawyers do not like their clients. Some lawyers describe their clients as stupid or dumb, or eccentric or belligerent, greedy or even crooked. I once represented clients who felt the only way we were going to win their case was to bribe a witness or even the judge. Although I informed them, in no uncertain terms, that is not the way the system worked, they did not believe me. I debated severing my relationship with them (a husband and wife) but did not. They had a good case and deservedly were entitled to damages. We ultimately settled it, but I will truthfully say I never did like those clients.

It is easy to become frustrated with some clients. Clients are just people. As a professional a lawyer must learn to recognize a client's human fallibility as well as the positive and likeable characteristics. Clients will be markedly different from lawyers and judges. They have not grown up under the law or even been exposed to legal ethics. As such, they not only need the lawyer's guidance, but they require as well the lawyer's understanding of their frustrations, needs and weaknesses. In the law, they only know what they read or see dramatized on television. They may act as if they know, but the truth is, they are insecure. They require not only the lawyer's legal help, but many clients look to their lawyer as their newly found confidant to help them with life's most difficult decisions. Divorce clients need someone to counsel with on nonlegal issues. Those clients that are injured need the lawyer's confidence to keep them going. In short, all clients need their lawyer's friendship. The problem remains for the lawyer; friendship is difficult to offer to any person if you don't like them. If the client is in bankruptcy and you are trying to protect what little assets you can, the client may not trust you without the lawyer showing the utmost interest in the client's desperate financial plight. All client's have emotional problems; after all, they are only human. The schizophrenic needs more understanding than those that are emotionally stable.

Lawyers often are frustrated over the fact that clients cannot supply through their testimony the essential legal element to make a case. In the zeal to win, I have observed cases where it becomes obvious lawyers have attempted to manipulate their clients to get them to shade the truth. The short response to this is that it is, and always will be, subornation of perjury. The client may not know that and often times will go along simply because the lawyer has convinced them that it is the truth. Under these circumstances, the lawyer has more to lose than the client.

In representing any client, it is essential that counsel seek the utmost confidence by the client in what counsel advises and in the manner in which counsel conducts the case. Of course, the converse of this situation governs as well; counsel must have confidence in the client and in the client's version of the case. A relationship must be established that clients will *truthfully* reveal the weakness of their case as well as their strengths. Failure to do so can lead to irreparable harm. I always told clients they should assume the other side knows everything about them and failure to reveal to me any adverse information would defeat their case.

The Client's Best Interest

Lawyers should always put the best interests of their client as the primary goal. Sometimes occasions may arise where it is best to persuade the client not to pursue the lawsuit if there can be resultant emotional harm to the client involved.

Years ago a couple came to me to file suit against an obstetrician. They were of Greek nationality. They had no children. They were forty years of age and had been trying to have a child ever since they were married in their early twenties. A year before the wife had visited her doctor, having missed her period. The doctor told her the news she so much wanted to hear. She was pregnant. This was such a momentous event in their life. They called in all their friends and relatives and held a three day party. Gifts were brought. Relatives traveled from Greece to help celebrate this blessed event. Thereafter, the expectant mother went on regular visits into her obstetrician's office. She never saw the doctor. She was checked by the nurse. She was given medicine to protect against any possible hemorrhaging. Her periodic examinations were deemed to be normal. She thought it odd that she did not show or feel the baby; she was reassured by the nurse that some pregnant people often do not look pregnant; that it was nothing to worry about. Two weeks before she was scheduled to deliver, she saw the nurse who called the doctor who told her that he wanted her to go to the hospital for an x-ray. She did. The tragic news was revealed; she never had been pregnant. There was a mistaken diagnosis. She collapsed in the doctor's office. Thereafter, she had a complete mental breakdown. She underwent psychiatric care and was hospitalized for six months.

She had a good malpractice case. I felt the case worth substantial money. We entered into a contingent fee contract. I knew her psychiatrist; he was a reputable doctor. I arranged for an appointment with him. He told me that the young woman had suffered an emotional injury that was acute. She was still under his care and was still depressed. She had been borderline psychotic. He cautioned me. It was his opinion that filing the lawsuit and the woman's submission to a deposition causing her to relive her emotional experience could cause a reoccurrence of her mental trauma such that she could become permanently disabled. I called the husband into the office. I told him what the psychiatrist had told me. I told him that I thought it would be a tragic mistake to subject his wife to the emotional trauma which would be caused by the lawsuit. He agreed. We never filed the case.

In another unusual case, two young mothers had traveled to Nebraska from another state to attend a national convention. They were both married and each had three beautiful children. The last night of the convention, they decided to celebrate. They both had too much to drink. Three young men picked them up at a bar. It was the mistake of their lifetime. It cost them their lives. They were found the next morning in a vehicle wrapped around a tree outside of town. The driver was drunk. The young mothers and two boys, all in the back seat, were killed. The driver lived. Two years later, I was called by an outstate lawyer where the surviving husbands lived with the surviving children. He told me he had two good wrongful death cases. The husbands visited me. I agreed to investigate the case. I called the insurance company and they offered to let me review their investigative file. I gained information that had never been publicly revealed. Both of the mothers were found partially clad. They had spent the night on a lake beach with the three young boys who had consensual sex with each of them. The insurance company said they would not pay anything in the case and felt that a jury would not award damages. I consulted with the referring lawyer and with one of the surviving husbands. I told him I thought liability was a major problem, but I was more concerned whether the husbands and their children would want a public trial revealing what these young women had done. The young men were not innocent, but two of them had paid with their lives. It was my recommendation that the case not be filed. I told them the choice was theirs, but I did not believe I wanted to participate in it. I felt the emotional trauma to the survivors would be too great. They ultimately agreed.

My point is that I think attorneys need to be morally concerned with the personal well-being of their clients. As I told the young fathers, "money is secondary" to the emotional trauma that could follow. The pecuniary interests of both the lawyer and client should always be secondary to the well-being of the client.

Consulting With The Client

As I indicated, lawyers sometimes forget that it is the client's case and not theirs. I do not say this in denigration of the lawyer because more often than not problems of this nature arise simply because a lawyer becomes so busy or engaged in the litigation process that in the heat of the moment he or she slights the fact that it is the client's cause and interest that is involved. The following anecdote is illustrative of communications problems between counsel and client.

When I started practice, our firm had a young associate with approximately five years experience who was responsible for processing twenty or more files for a major insurance company. He had been taking depositions, filing pleadings, and making preliminary arguments on motions in these cases.

One day one of the senior partners received a wire from the insurance company directing him to take all of the company's files that our firm was handling and deliver them to another law firm. The senior partner immediately called the claims attorney for the company in Chicago and found out that for the past year and a half the company had made repeated inquiries about the progress and status of all of the cases that were being handled by the associate and had never received a reply.

The senior partner flew to Chicago for a conference with the insurance company's general counsel. They agreed that the associate would be relieved of his duties. The client would not transfer the files. They would be taken over by the senior partner. Our firm handled the files to completion, but it was quickly apparent that the insurance company had stopped sending us new files. We later learned that new cases were being directed to another law firm.

Some lawyers fail to keep their clients informed about the progress of the case. This can cause a great many problems—needless frustration for the client, false steps in the litigation, or, as related, the loss of the client.

The Client's Role On Strategic Decisions

The failure of counsel to consult with the client about strategic decisions during a lawsuit is a mistake. For example, in the criminal law it is essential that the client make the ultimate decisions on whether to plead guilty, whether the trial should proceed before a jury or a judge, or whether he or she should take the witness stand. The lawyer should, of course, make recommendations. The problem is that often the lawyer's understanding of legal proceedings provides a basis for making strategic decisions but the client lacks that same knowledge and base understanding.

The failure to consult on strategic decisions is a drastic mistake. Lawyers can explain to their client the legal considerations that lie behind the choices and judgments that have to be made so that the client can participate in the decision to the extent of their desire and ability. In the vast majority of cases, the client is willing to go along with the lawyer's recommendation.

Consultation with the client can avoid malpractice claims against the lawyer. I have noticed that many medical malpractice cases are initiated when the doctor fails to maintain good relations and rapport with the patient. I recall a claim from a woman who was operated on by a skillful surgeon for an injury to the facial nerve. Months later, the patient returned to the neurosurgeon to complain that she could not open her left eye. The doctor looked at her and said, "I don't remember operating on you; go to your family physician." Rather than going to the family physician, she came to my office to file a malpractice case.

This person's case presents a lesson that all lawyers should heed as well. The client should fully understand what the lawyer is doing, win or lose, and feel he or she has received good representation. The lawyer should always be willing to consult with the client and answer any question.

Overstating The Likelihood Of Success To The Client

There is a natural tendency for lawyers during initial meetings with prospective clients to overstate the prospects of a favorable result. After all, lawyers hope to persuade prospective clients to retain them. The lawyer should never intentionally misrepresent the chances of success to a client. The reputation of all lawyers depends on doing professional work for each client. Whether or not a client returns, or whether or not a client will recommend the lawyer to others in the community, depends a great deal upon the client's attitude at the conclusion of the case. Lawyers should not forget that this attitude is often dependent upon expectations established in the initial discussions with a lawyer.

Some lawyers file lawsuits seeking huge recoveries far in excess of the realistic value of the case. This strategy can backfire when the case comes to trial if the defense lawyer calls attention to the jury that the plaintiff is demanding hundreds of thousands of dollars for a very minor injury. Jurors may think that if plaintiff's counsel is unfair about one part of his case, the lawyer is probably unfair about other matters as well.

Praying for too much money in the complaint can have other negative effects. On behalf of one of our clients who had a serious injury, we sued for damages in excess of One Hundred Thousand Dollars. Before trial, however, we discovered a serious problem in proving liability, and I recommended settlement at Twenty-five Thousand Dollars. The client refused. He thought that the damages, as prayed, stated the actual value of his injury. Despite my explanation of the obvious, he refused to budge. We were forced to trial. We almost lost the case on the liability and the damages awarded were less than for what we could have settled. Our client was never satisfied.

These situations can result in more harm to the lawyer than good. If the client has an inflated value in mind, he or she will often be dissatisfied even if the case is settled for a realistic value. I learned my lesson and always discussed with my clients the amount of money sought in the complaint before commencing suit. Some jurisdictions prohibit lawyers from pleading a specific amount of damages. Perhaps this is the better approach because the amount of the damages for which suit is brought is seldom the amount that will actually be awarded.

Understating The Value Of The Case To The Client

I have discussed the problem of overstating the case, but it is important not to understate it, either. I learned this lesson when I was recommended to represent a staff sergeant in the Air Force who was struck by a car while walking in the crosswalk across a city street.

The sergeant told me that he had not observed the car approach. I mentioned to him my concern that the other side would try to prove that he had not looked before crossing the intersection. His failure to see that which was in plain sight could be construed as negligence as a matter of law and could bar recovery. My client was outraged. He stated he had been hit by the car, that the driver of the vehicle was clearly liable and there should not be any question in recovering for his injury. I did my best to tell him that I felt he should receive a substantial recovery, but I wanted him to understand the realistic risks we faced.

The sergeant signed a contingent fee contact authorizing me to represent him. Two days later I picked up the local newspaper and read that he had filed his lawsuit by another lawyer. I received a registered letter discharging me. I immediately called my client. He said, "Well, I started to think about what you told me. I didn't think that you had sufficient confidence in my case. You were concerned we might lose the case and I wanted someone who believed in me."

This was a lesson I never forgot.

The Client Discharges The Lawyer

I was once asked to represent a hospitalized man who was struck by a car driven by a prominent city councilman.

On the police report, the officer mentioned that the elderly councilman wore thick glasses and had not seen the pedestrian crossing the street. Although it was seldom done, I recommended to my client that we attach to our complaint a motion to have an immediate eye examination of the defendant. I thought that it would provide a psychological edge in getting a fair settlement in the case. The client agreed and we entered into a written contract that evening which was based upon a one-third contingent fee.

I was in the process of drafting the complaint later in the week. Before I could get it filed, I received a letter from the client discharging me. The astonishing thing was that a newspaper report the next day stated that a suit had been filed on his behalf and attached to the complaint was a motion by the plaintiff seeking an eye examination of the defendant. I called the client and he told me that another lawyer had been referred to him by a friend and that the lawyer had offered to handle the case on a twenty-five percent basis rather than the one-third fee.

What to do? Every client has a right to discharge a lawyer, and hire another one. However, in this case, I felt the other lawyer had solicited the case on an unethical basis, and in addition had literally stolen my work product in filing the motion for an eye examination. It was the only time in my career that I filed a lien for attorney fees in a case. The lien prevented the defendant from settling the lawsuit without discharge of my lien. When the case was finally settled, the lawyer reluctantly paid me a share of the attorney fee.

Investigate The Client's Case Before You File Suit

One day a middle aged woman from Chicago came to see me in my office. She said four years ago she was traveling on a Greyhound bus which had temporarily stopped in Omaha. When she entered the lavatory in the bus station, she fell on a poorly marked step and struck her eye against a counter. She lost her eye and now used a glass eye. She had been trying to settle her claim with the Union Pacific Railway, which then handled all Greyhound litigation. The four-year statute of limitation would run at the end of the month.

I told her I would look into her case and would call her the next day at her hotel. When she left, I called the General Counsel at the Union Pacific. He told me that my prospective client had been represented by Jim Dooley, then a noted trial lawyer in Chicago, but he had withdrawn from the case. He said that the woman was a fraud.

The General Counsel offered to allow me to review his file, which was about two feet high and reflected four years of discussions. I asked him to relate the contents of the file. He said the woman had been in the Army and ten years before had put her eye out in a military accident. The VA Hospital in Denver had treated her for several years. The General Counsel felt the woman was psychotic.

My five minute phone call saved much time, expense and embarrassment. Of course, I refused to take her case. She later hired another lawyer who without investigation immediately filed suit in federal district court. The lawyer took several pictures of the restroom and commenced discovery. I read about the suit in the paper and called the lawyer. He didn't believe me, but ultimately withdrew. Unbelievably, the woman proceeded to trial pro se, that is, she represented herself. After three days of trial, the trial court dismissed the case.

PLEADING AND THE CLIENT

Consulting With Your Client As To What You Plead

I have often observed factual averments pled in either complaints or answers that are inconsistent with the client's story. Depending on the procedural law of the forum, the client may need to sign and even swear to the pleadings. This is not true in federal court. Lawyers often carelessly plead factual details without consulting their client. I have known lawyers whose clients executed detached sworn affidavits as to the truth of the pleadings and only later did the lawyer actually draft the factual pleading to be attached to the client's sworn signature. In one case, the client testified that he had signed a blank affidavit in order to explain the factual variance between his testimony and the pleading filed. The lawyer was terribly embarrassed. It is little wonder in situations like this that parties (plaintiffs or defendants) are impeached by the contradictory factual statements pleaded by their own counsel. The client usually is telling the truth, but is made to appear to be untruthful by his or her own lawyer. *Never forget to consult with your client as to what you plead, and make certain what you plead reflects the client's actual recollection of the facts.* In most states a client's pleading can constitute an admission against interest.

The Difficult Client

One of the most troublesome cases that I handled involved an immigrant who understood little English.

She was injured while standing at a street corner waiting for a local bus to take her to work. The intersection was two blocks away from the stockyards. That morning a rancher delivered a large bull to the stockyard. Someone had left open a gate and the bull escaped. The bull ran onto a sidewalk where it spied my client wearing bright clothing. The bull ran her down and crushed her shoulder in several places.

My client's collar bone had to be surgically replaced. She was left with a permanent disability. During the course of her treatment, the surgeon performed seven additional procedures unrelated to the shoulder injury. We knew this woman's many ailments would make it difficult to prove that the shoulder injury caused her total disability. We also were concerned whether we could prove who was at fault. It was going to be difficult to prove whether the stockyard or the rancher, or both, were responsible for the open gate.

From the very beginning I realized that my client did not understand the legal proceedings. When the trial began, the two defendants offered her Thirty Thousand Dollars. I recommended that she take the offer. However, she said she would take it solely on the condition that if she had further doctor bills and further surgery, which she said she needed, the defendants would also agree to pay those costs without limitation.

Of course, this was impossible. I did my best to explain this to her on repeated occasions. I also retained an independent physician to assure her that no further surgeries were indicated. We hired an interpreter, but it did little good. Each time we had settlement discussions, I felt she would agree to the offer but she refused unless I could assure her that all of her future bills for the rest of her life would be paid.

The trial proceeded. After three days the defendants increased their offer to Fifty Thousand Dollars. I thought this was a very fair offer. But the client still would not settle. I asked the judge if he would visit with her and explain to her exactly what the situation was. After about a forty-five minute discussion with the judge, she appeared to agree to settle. I suggested to the judge that we have a judgment entered in open court so that there could be no misunderstanding about it. I asked the client on the record if she was satisfied with the offer. She then repeated, "Only if they pay all of my medical bills for the rest of my life." We were totally exasperated and didn't know what to do. The trial proceeded.

That evening I visited the client's home and talked to her husband. He agreed that we should settle the case. The next day I made the announcement in open court that a judgment for Fifty Thousand Dollars was being entered and the money would be paid into the court. I again wanted it on the record that the plaintiff was present and would accept. I asked the husband if this was agreeable with him (he was a party to the suit as well) and he answered it was. I asked the plaintiff if she would so accept. She stood mute. I then said in the presence of the court: "The plaintiff is present with her husband and he has stated the settlement is satisfactory." I wasn't certain the wife understood what was going on, but I didn't know what else to do.

The final sad twist to all of this is that the money was paid into the clerk's office to satisfy the judgment. The check was written payable to both the husband and the wife, and my name appeared on the check as their attorney. The problem was that we could not get the plaintiff to come in to satisfy the judgment and take her money. No one received any money for almost a year and a half. Finally a friend of the plaintiff explained the situation to her and she took the steps necessary for receiving her cash.

Looking back on the situation, I think it might have been better to have appointed a guardian to represent the plaintiff. However, I'm not certain that would have been possible. It certainly would have helped alleviate the serious problem at the end of the trial. The lesson to be learned from all of this is that the lawyer must be cognizant of the client's lack of knowledge of the legal process and must do everything possible to reassure the client that the case is moving appropriately along. This may take extra time. However, if the relationship between client and lawyer is to be meaningful, it is essential that the lawyer educate the client about the legal process and the risks of litigation.

The Egg Case

I once represented a woman in a malpractice case against a dentist, who had filled and capped her teeth. For whatever reason, the dentist had placed permanent caps over obvious cavities. Subsequent x-rays demonstrated this. My client suffered infection and severe pain. We were able to work out a settlement with the dentist's insurance carrier. When the releases were executed, my client went to the grocery store and bought a dozen eggs. She plastered the dentist's waiting room walls with the raw eggs. Her psychiatrist called me and told me she was a schizophrenic and he blamed me for the egg incident. I told him that I was in the dark about her emotional illness. However, I thought even the mentally ill deserved proper dental care.

A few years later the same woman came to me to represent her in an automobile accident claim. She claimed she had a severe back injury which caused her to walk with a limp. I contacted her orthopedic doctor. His report said she suffered a back sprain in the accident, but she had fully recovered. He opined that her limp was from polio she had contracted as a child and had nothing to do with her accident. The woman wanted me to sue for a large sum. I showed her the orthopedic doctor's report and finally convinced her to settle for a nominal amount without suit. Unknown to me, when she got her check she headed to the orthopaedic doctor's office with another supply of raw eggs. Fortunately, the receptionist intercepted her and sent her over to her psychiatrist in the same building. The psychiatrist called me once again and lectured me for showing her the orthopedic report. This time he was probably right, but she had a right to know I had no evidence to prove her claim.

Whatever The Cost, The Attorney-Client Privilege Must Be Honored

I had a divorce case in which the father of my client was a lawyer. I had tried many cases against him and our relationship was not always pleasant. One day he came to my office and asked me if I would be willing to represent his daughter in her divorce. I told him I was honored that he would ask me to represent her. The lawyer assured me that the daughter was *my* client and he would not get involved in the case. Of course, I responded that I appreciated his confidence but I would solicit any advice that he might make as the case progressed.

The lawyer told me his son-in-law was a "bum." After I interviewed the daughter, I came to share his appraisal. The husband had a narcissistic complex. He was guilty of physically abusing his wife. When he arrived home from work he would fly into a rage and literally beat up his wife if he found an ashtray out of place or a bed not made. This abuse caused my client to have a nervous breakdown requiring her to be hospitalized.

I filed suit for divorce and obtained a restraining order to prevent the husband from going into the home or contacting his wife in any way. She unquestionably had legitimate grounds for divorce. Our basic concern was whether we could discover all of the property and assets that the husband had. He had a good job, and my client felt he had more money than he had revealed to her. She knew he had at least one or two hidden investments.

The husband's lawyer and I had litigated many cases against each other, and had a practice of arranging for a convenient, mutual date for both parties to appear for their depositions on a back-to-back basis. I was about ready to take the deposition of the defendant when I told my client she would also have to appear and give her deposition. At that point she told me something that she thought I should know.

Before confiding in me, she first sought my utmost promise that I would not reveal the information to her father because "it would break his heart." I assured her that because she was my client, the attorney-client privilege prevented me from repeating what she told me. She then related information that not only was embarrassing to her but would also seriously prejudice her case. In addition, she revealed that in the past few weeks, she had observed a car continually following her. It was not difficult for me to discern that the defense was aware of her activities. I could only assume her husband's lawyer had gathered investigative details that would embarrass my client at her deposition. I stressed that she must cease any conduct which could affect her case.

My client's revelation became my primary challenge. Counsel for her husband often saw me and said: "Any time you want to take my client's deposition, let me know, but be sure and bring along your client because I want to take her deposition as well." I could not put her under oath and let her be subjected to humiliating questions. Her father insisted on going to the depositions.

I decided that I could not allow the depositions to proceed; I began to make my first overtures to settle the case. In the meantime, the father began questioning the delay in deposing the husband. I informed him that I was on top of everything. I stated I was conducting some quiet investigations and that I believed the depositions would at this time prejudice discovering all of the information. The father insisted that the only way that the case could be favorably settled was by placing the husband under oath and taking his deposition. I continued to delay. After each call from the father, the daughter would call wanting reassurance that her father would never know about what she had revealed to me.

Finally we resolved the case with a reasonable settlement. I must admit that it was not the best settlement, but I was confident that if I had gone to trial the court would have given my client less because of her misconduct. Her misconduct might even have prevented her from obtaining the divorce. I filed for what I considered a reasonable fee, which was to be paid by the husband. The husband's counsel indicated his client would contest the fee. My client's father volunteered to testify for the other side; he contended I was entitled to little or no fee. He even wrote the state bar association seeking discipline because of my ethical failure to pursue the case diligently. Without revealing my client's confidence, I was able to turn aside the complaint to the ethics committee and the district court awarded me the reasonable fee requested.

This was a situation with no easy solutions. The bottom line, however, is that the attorney-client privilege must always be honored.

THE ATTORNEY FEE

To Fee Or Not To Fee

This may seem like a silly question. Of course, the lawyer's time is all that he has to sell, and it is essential that the lawyer have a reasonable fee schedule to maintain his office overhead and a reasonable income. However, in every lawyer's practice, there can be situations in which the fee should be waived or reduced based upon the time expended and the result reached.

Lawyers for individuals often charge a fee if they recover for their clients. Their contingency fee is a percentage of the recovery. England and most of the European countries outlaw the use of contingent fee arrangements. Most civil law countries have adopted shifting fee systems in which the losing party must pay the winning party's fees.

The "loser pays" system denies access to the courts by poor and middle class individuals who cannot take the risk in bringing a suit even if their claim is justifiable. I was in Thailand a few years ago and my young guide had been in a serious automobile accident in which the driver of the other car had gone to sleep. She was told that if she brought a lawsuit she might be thrown into debt if she lost her case. Rather than face that risk, she settled for her medical expenses, even though she is disabled for life. Of course, if she had lived in a country with a contingent fee system, this would not have happened.

I have always maintained that the contingent fee system is the most fair and equitable system because most lawyers will not take a case unless they feel there is a likelihood of success. Few lawyers will accept contingency fee cases in which they anticipate token recoveries after expenditure of a great deal of time. On this basis the contingent fee system serves to deter lawyers from taking frivolous cases.

Charging No Fee

I recall a minister from a rural church coming to me. His left leg was paralyzed. He had been making calls in the country late one evening and had approached a railroad crossing. The crossing had no warning signals other than the crossbar. Because of the infrequency and the irregular schedule of trains, he had crossed the track many times without concern about approaching trains. On the evening in question, he crossed the track at a moderate rate of speed. He hit the twentieth car behind the engine and was crushed in his car.

After I investigated I told the minister that under existing state law there was no possibility of winning the case. He had a duty to stop for approaching trains. I suggested he allow me to try to negotiate a settlement without filing a law suit. I would draft a complaint alleging a dangerous crossing. However, I told him I would not file the lawsuit because I felt that it would be too difficult to prove liability.

With the minister's permission, I made an appointment with the general attorney for the railroad and showed him the draft complaint. The moderate settlement we negotiated did not come close to compensating the minister for his injuries, but it was the best that I could do for him. I did not charge him a fee.

Charging A Reduced Fee

Lawyers must also make a judgment about how much to charge. If you spend little time on the case, it is sensible not to charge a full fee. I recall a case in which I was asked to assist two women who were hit by a driver who crossed over the center line of the highway.

The driver was a rabbi who lived in Denver, Colorado. He suffered minor injuries. The two women were hospitalized in a little town in Kansas, where the accident occurred. I interviewed the women at the hospital a week after the accident. I told them that I felt each had a good claim worth a great deal of money. The most important question was how much insurance the other driver had because that would determine in all probability how much the women would receive.

We investigated the scene of the accident. I found eye glasses that were laying in the grass off the shoulder of the road. I flew to Denver the next day and went to the rabbi's home. He had reported the accident to his company but did not have a lawyer. I introduced myself and told him who I was. I showed him the eye glasses. He said they were his (as I assumed). He was pleased to have them returned. He and his family were just sitting down to an evening meal and asked me to join them.

The rabbi had no money. He stated he did not know how he was going to pay for his own bills and that his car was completely totalled. I asked him if he had collision damage and he did not understand what that was. I felt sure that under his insurance policy he had medical coverage that would take care of his own bills. I told him that if he would show me his insurance policy, I might be able to explain. He produced it and I found that he had insurance coverage which provided liability insurance up to Twenty Thousand Dollars for each of my clients. He was relieved to find he did have medical coverage for his own bills and he did have collision insurance. I told him that he should consult with his own insurance company about the medical coverage and his collision. I thanked him for the time and flew back home.

I immediately wrote a letter to the insurance company and told them that I represented the two women. I described my clients' severe damages (I had two medical reports), and opined that their damages would be well in excess of One Hundred Thousand Dollars. I informed the company that I knew that the rabbi, its insured, had coverage of Twenty Thousand Dollars per person, if the company would be willing to pay the full amount of the coverage immediately I would not commence a suit. A few days later, the company agreed to my offer. Within two weeks time I had a check for Twenty Thousand Dollars for each of the women. I took it down to my clients in the hospital in Kansas and told them that my charge would be the amount of my plane fare and One Thousand Dollars each for my time. This was agreeable with the referring lawyer.

This was the kind of case where lawyers can serve their clients without charging large fees. The clients will remember your assistance. When their friends or family have legal difficulties, they will refer cases to you. In fact, this happened in this very situation at a later time.

Referral Cases

Referral cases from other lawyers who did not try cases often make up a substantial part of a trial lawyer's docket. It is important to consider that the referring lawyer is a "client" too. The same rules relating to communication, talking over strategy and keeping the referring lawyer informed are applicable to this situation as with any other client. It is good for one's business in not only ethically justifying the referring lawyer's fee split "for services rendered," but it is helpful in dealing with the actual litigant. Often times the litigant has greater confidence in his or her own lawyer than they do to the lawyer to whom the case is referred for trial. In dealing with referral lawyers, however, difficulties can often arise on the division of the fee. Make certain the lawyer referring the case fully understands in advance the fee arrangement. It is a good idea to have the arrangement spelled out in writing.

Don't Be Greedy

One time lawyers from another state referred a serious personal injury case to me for filing suit in the federal court in my home state. They agreed I should receive two-thirds of the attorney's fees for taking, filing and trying the case and they were to receive one-third. After filing the complaint, I took several depositions, interviewed the respective doctors for each side, and worked up the case. On the eve of trial we made a very substantial settlement. I processed the check, provided the client his share, and sent the one-third fee to the attorneys in the other state. The referring lawyers responded that since the case had been settled before trial the fee should be divided equally between our two law firms. I replied the insurance company knew our firm would go to trial unless a fair offer was received. Experienced defense lawyers often value cases on whether the lawyer on the plaintiff's side will *always* settle the case. Many plaintiff lawyers have that reputation. We did not. We had undertaken a great deal of discovery work and they had done little more than refer the case. On this basis, I felt that the original arrangement was still appropriate. The lawyers threatened me with a lawsuit and wrote nasty letters, but I remained firm. Nothing more came of the matter.

The converse of that situation occurred in connection with a referral from lawyers in Paris, France. A young woman from Pennsylvania who was working as a civilian employee for the Army near Paris was severely injured in a car accident with another civilian employee from Nebraska. The Paris lawyers sent me a huge box with statements taken from Army employees, French Police, and many, many pictures. They had thoroughly investigated the case but had been unsuccessful in getting the case settled without filing the lawsuit.

I brought suit in federal court. After the first deposition, defense counsel made me a very substantial and reasonable offer. I recommended it to the client. She approved. I called the referring lawyers in Paris and they felt the offer should be accepted.

Once again, the referral was based on the usual fee arrangement of one-third referral fee and the two-thirds to me. I sent the Paris lawyers fifty percent of the fee. I told them I thought they had performed as much or more work than I had. Their response was overwhelming. They wrote that they had never before received *more* than the agreed upon amount. They promised to refer to me any future cases they had in the United States. And they did. The moral of the story is if "you spread a little bread on the water," it often pays many dividends.

Whatever Happens, Be Ethical

As I have indicated, I always believed that the ethics code required that in order to share a fee with another firm, the referring lawyer should perform some concrete services for the client. Whenever possible, I asked the referring lawyer to come to court with me or to appear with me at depositions. This also helped to bolster the client's confidence because the client's primary relationship was with the referring lawyer.

One local lawyer had sent me some cases over a three or four year period. One time, however, he called me and said an insurance company had forwarded a claim to defend but he couldn't handle the matter because he represented the workmen's compensation carrier for the decedent-plaintiff. The employee had been killed while in a construction accident, and the workmen's compensation carrier had paid benefits to the decedent's estate. It could recover the amounts it had paid if the decedent's estate prevailed in its suit with the insurance company.

Under these circumstances, the referring lawyer told me that he had a conflict of interest and was not able to handle the defense of the case. He recommended me to the insurance company and the insurance company directly retained me. I filed an appropriate answer and engaged in discovery. Because of the excessive demand by the plaintiff's lawyer, I was unable to settle the case. After two weeks of the trial, the jury returned a defendant's verdict and the plaintiff received nothing.

I billed my fee to the insurance company based upon my hourly rate. Thereafter, I received a call from the lawyer who had recommended me. He said "I am coming over to get my usual one-third referral fee on the case you defended." I told the lawyer that I did not understand the arrangement that way. I was deeply concerned that any division of the fee would be unethical because he had represented the workmen's compensation carrier and had sat during the trial on the plaintiff's side of the table. Although he had not actually tried the case for the other side, he had served as co-counsel and consulted with the plaintiff's counsel throughout the case. He had earlier agreed that he had a conflict of interest, so I could not understand how it would be ethical for us to share the fee.

The other lawyer made my life miserable for the next two months. He went to many of my friends. They all advised me I should share the fee. The lawyer even went to the minister of my church and complained that I was unethical because I had not given him his fair share of the fee. The minister called me to suggest that I pay up. I thanked him for the consultation but I pointed out to him, as I did to my friends, it was unethical to be on two sides of the case at the same time. As far as I was concerned, it was not the money involved but the ethics governing the situation. I felt that if I shared the fee I could be found to be equally unethical as the referring lawyer.

CHAPTER III
ADVOCACY BEFORE TRIAL

INTRODUCTION

INVESTIGATING THE CASE
Investigation Of The Facts Is Not Only To Determine How An Event Happened, But To Find Out Whether The Recollection And Recordation Of The Facts Is Reliable

Gathering The Evidence

Lay Investigators Do Not Understand The Rules of Evidence

Evidence Can Be Found In Unusual Places

THE FACTS ARE NOT ALWAYS WHAT THEY APPEAR TO BE
The Air Force Court Martial Board

The Covered-Up Ditch

The Bogus Doctor Bills

The Misleading Photos

The Misleading X-ray

The Phoney Doctor

PLEADING YOUR CASE
Consider The Consequences Of What You Plead

What You Plead Determines What Can Be Proven

General Denials Can Open Pandora's Box

Do Not Plead More Than Is Necessary

The Evil Of Pleading Legal Conclusions

DISCOVERY

The Purpose Of Discovery

Working With Difficult Lawyers

Handling "The Discovery Nut"

Calculating Discovery

Interrogatories

Depositions

Motions To Produce

DEMONSTRATIVE EVIDENCE

Too Much Or Too Little

Converting The Opponent's Evidence

THE PRETRIAL CONFERENCE

Every Trial Counsel Should Insist On A Pretrial Conference

NEGOTIATION

Valuating Your Case

Your Client's Case Is Unique

Whatever You Do, Be Fair And Realistic

Reasonable "Puffing"

INTRODUCTION

There is a popular myth that advocacy occurs only in the court-room. However, this myth overlooks the basic definition of advocacy from Webster's (or whatever source) which defines advocacy as the process of "pleading" or persuasion in the cause of another. Many lawyers fail to appreciate that advocacy begins the first time they meet their prospective clients. The purpose of this chapter is to discuss the human process as it relates to the initial interviews as well as some of the other important phases of litigation a lawyer confronts before trial.

INVESTIGATING THE CASE

Investigation Of The Facts Is Not Only To Determine How An Event Happened, But To Find Out Whether The Recollection And Recordation Of The Facts Is Reliable

Obviously, the facts must be favorable to the client's case or the client will lose. The lawyer must be reconciled to the existing facts: in other words, counsel must play the hand as it was dealt. *The lawyer's primary responsibility is to investigate how facts are recalled and recorded.* Years ago in his famous treatise "Courts on Trial," Jerome Frank theorized about "fact skepticism." He pointed out that witnesses tend to view factual occurrences in different ways. The interest of the witness may often serve to color this viewpoint. For example, X says that the intersection collision with Y was Y's fault because Y ran a red light. Y, on the other hand, says that X ran the red light. One of the two is wrong. However, the above events might be interpreted in a different way by a neutral witness, A, who a year later attempts to recall what was observed. Jurors may well interpret A's testimony in diverse ways depending on A's mannerisms and ability to recall what A observed. Under these circumstances, *the best means society has developed to ascertain "the truth" is through the adversary system with competing interests to be evaluated by "neutral" factfinders to determine which interest deserves recognition.* Although many observers, including lawyers and judges, fault the adversary system, no one has come up with a better idea to test possible human error in determining what is truth.

The value to be gained from Jerome Frank's observation is that the lawyer cannot be overly concerned with how the actual occurrence took place. Rather the lawyer must constantly consider how the available documentary and oral recollections can be converted into admissible evidence which will persuade the neutral factfinder to find "the facts" in favor of his client. In pursuing this role, the primary objective of the investigation is to determine the reliability of the investigative facts.

Gathering The Evidence

Obviously, *how* the evidence of past events is collected is of paramount importance. The question "how" depends for the most part on who is assigned the task of gathering the evidence. In most instances, the lawyers retained to represent the client will have the major responsibility. However, busy lawyers often will delegate this task to assistants and more often than not to lay investigators. While understandable, by delegating the investigative tasks, the lawyer loses the close contact with the developing factual scenario. One of the problems many lawyers confront is that they may be retained well after the incident giving rise to the lawsuit and the lapse of significant time may well impair memories, making the actual facts difficult to recreate.

Lay Investigators Do Not Understand The Rules Of Evidence

Years ago on separate occasions I represented two different insurance companies who had insured apartment house owners for damages arising from injuries incurred on the premises. In the first case, a tenant claimed that her hair was caught in the wringer bars of a washing machine furnished by the owners of the building for use by the tenant. The tenant had immediately hit the release safety button, but the wringer did not release and her hair was pulled into the machine causing her serious injury. She claimed that the release mechanism had rusted and was not in proper working condition. The adjustor inspected the machine and found no rust. He told the landlord to keep the machine for the trial so the jury could inspect it. When I came into the case, I visited the landlord to view the machine and found that the landlord had stored the machine in an outdoor garage. The entire machine was completely rusted and could not be used in evidence.

In a second similar case, a young woman had caught her hand in the wringer bar. The release button did not work. She claimed the release mechanism did not work properly. The insured was told to keep the machine for evidence. When I visited the landlord, I found the wringer bar taken apart. The landlord had oiled it and reassembled it so that it would function perfectly at trial.

In both cases, the investigators failed properly to preserve the machines for *evidence* at trial.

Evidence Can Be Found In Unusual Places

Evidence can be often discovered through exhausting the least obvious sources. Lawyers should go further than simply interviewing witnesses on official reports. Door to door canvassing of neighborhoods may turn up pertinent facts. One of my clients received a severe head concussion after a serious accident. Her automobile was severely damaged, indicating that the other automobile had been travelling at a high rate of speed. No witnesses were reported on the official accident reports. After the defendant's insurance company refused to settle, I filed suit. My client, who was a young woman, had complete amnesia and could not testify about the accident. I went door to door in the neighborhood looking for witnesses. A housewife two doors from the corner where the accident occurred said she was inside her kitchen and heard the crash but did not see it. She did remember, however, that the city garbage truck was in her driveway picking up garbage at the time. I went to the garbage company, obtained the roster of the workmen working the neighborhood that day, and located two city employees who had observed the accident. Both gave me sworn statements, which I sent to the insurance company. The company paid us the full insurance coverage without trial.

THE FACTS ARE NOT ALWAYS WHAT THEY APPEAR TO BE

Several cases on which I have worked illustrated the point that the facts as they first appear may not reveal the whole story. These cases reinforce the importance of thorough witness interviews.

The Air Force Court Martial Board

My former partner and I represented the defendant in a manslaughter case brought before a Court Martial Board in the Air Force. I investigated the case. Our client and a fellow soldier were driving at an excessive rate of speed (estimated to be in excess of one hundred miles per hour) on a state highway at one o'clock in the morning. They rear-ended a farmer driving a pickup truck at a slow rate of speed. The farmer was thrown from the truck and died instantly. The other soldier was also thrown from the car and was instantly killed. Our client was pinned under the steering wheel.

In front of the farmer was a stalled vehicle, which four employees of a meat packing plant were pushing down the road. A passing motorist saw the four men pushing the truck and take some of the clothing and personal belongings from the deceased farmer laying on the highway. Grisly to say the least!

The Air Force initiated an official "line of duty" investigation. An officer was appointed to do the investigation. As counsel to the accused, I had a right to accompany the officer on the investigation. Based on the investigation, our client was charged with manslaughter. Everything pointed to our client's guilt. He and the other soldier had left the air base club for noncommissioned officers in a drunken condition.

However, as I noted above, appearances can be deceptive. Despite the fact that our client was pinned behind the steering wheel of his car, our client had no chest injuries. We located two guards who had been at the base gate the evening of the accident and who remembered our client and other soldiers leaving the base in the early morning hours. They reported that our client was passed out in the back seat of the car and the other soldier was driving. Based on these facts, my partner retained an automobile reconstruction expert and in response to a hypothetical question, he opined that upon impact, our client had been thrown from the back seat to the front and had been pinned under the steering wheel column. He opined that the other soldier who was killed was thrown out of the left front door when it opened upon impact. The Air Force Board of Officers acquitted our client. A miscarriage of justice? The Air Force Board of Officers did not think so.

The Covered-Up Ditch

I represented an individual whose vehicle went out of control, crossed over the center line, and hit a milk truck coming from the opposite direction. The passenger in my client's vehicle was killed and my client, who was driving, was permanently disabled. The police report stated that my client's vehicle went out of control. My client had amnesia. No one could determine the reason he had lost control of his vehicle. The milk truck driver saw nothing except the car crossing the center line into his path. The police report listed no other witnesses, but did say on their report: "two off-duty sheriff deputies arrived at the scene shortly after the accident but they did not observe the crash." I thought it was important to interview the two deputies. Both officers no longer worked for the sheriff's office. After I located and interviewed them, their testimony became critical. In place of the normal curb they had observed a ditch running parallel to the edge of the highway. They overheard one of the on-duty officers instruct the foreman of the contractor to "fill in the ditch before someone blames you for the accident." The two deputies both verified that they saw fresh tire tracks at the bottom of the ditch. It became obvious that our client's vehicle had run onto the curbing and into the ditch causing their vehicle to go out of control.

As it turned out, the contractor, who was a good friend of the police officers, had dug the ditch as he was laying a new driveway for an adjacent filling station. I sued the contractor, the service station (leased by a major gasoline company), and the owner of the property. During discovery, I requested the names of all of the contractor's crew working that day. The contractor's payroll records revealed names and address of about ten to twelve laborers who had been hired from the Union Hall. I interviewed each of them. No barricades had been erected to warn motorists of the ditch. Four of them revealed that they had been told by the police to fill in the ditch. They had just arrived at work (the accident was at 7:00 a.m.) and had not seen the accident. During the second week of trial, the driver received a substantial settlement.

The Bogus Doctor Bills

I was defending a large department store in a case in which a sales clerk, who was moving swiftly through the aisles within the store, ran into a three-year-old boy. The boy, who had been running between the aisles, fell into a glass show case. The glass broke and the boy cut his forehead. The child needed stitches, so the store's management offered to take the child and his mother to the hospital. The mother insisted that the child be taken in an ambulance. While waiting for the ambulance, the mother angrily threatened the clerk, stating she was going to get even with the clerk and the store and would sue the store for millions. The store offered the mother a settlement around $3,000. The mother refused the settlement, claiming the child was scarred for life, and sued the store.

At the trial, counsel for the plaintiff asked me to stipulate into evidence the hospital admissions record which stated the child had received six stitches in the forehead at the hospital on the day of the accident; plaintiff's counsel also asked me to stipulate to the fact that the medical bills were reasonable. Their requests were reasonable and the stipulation was entered. The doctor's bill, which was undated, was $300 for two visits. This seemed excessive to me. I asked plaintiff's counsel if the doctor would testify in court. He said he thought so, but was not sure because he had not been able to get ahold of him. I thought this was strange, and at noon I called the doctor's office. I told the doctor who I was and that because of the doctor-patient privilege I was not inquiring about the little boy's medical condition. I told him I simply wanted to verify the amount of the bill for the department store accident.

The doctor's response was totally unexpected. He said: "That child's mother is crazy and a crook. This boy fell out of a crib when he was six months old and had a concussion. That was five years ago. I have been trying to collect that bill ever since. I never saw the boy for the department store accident you have described. That woman is a liar." I asked the doctor if he could come to court that afternoon and tell the jury what he had told me. He said: "I would be more than glad to do so." He did. The boy and the mother did not show up the next day for final argument. It turned out that the boy's stitches were removed by an emergency room nurse at the hospital without charge. The little boy never was seen by any doctor for the incident at the department store.

The plaintiff's attorney showed great resiliency. In closing, he argued "the accident was still the department store's fault; that this was the child's case not the mother's; don't punish the child for the mother's indiscretion." The jury argued for two days. In a 10-2 verdict, they finally awarded the little boy $250. The two dissenting jurors felt the verdict should be zero.

THE FACTS ARE NOT ALWAYS WHAT THEY APPEAR TO BE

The Misleading Photos

In another trial two large bread company trucks collided head-on with one another on an open highway. Both drivers were killed. There were no eye witnesses. I had sued on behalf of one of the decedent's estate. The entire case had to be tried on circumstantial evidence. My theory was that the left front side of the defendant's truck had hit the middle of my client's truck, and that the collision had occurred in my client's lane of traffic. I was able to establish a sufficient case to go to the jury on the basis of circumstantial evidence consisting of skid marks and the physical damage to my client's truck. The highway patrolman's testimony was also favorable to my client's case, as he testified that the collision had taken place on my client's side of the highway.

The other side retained an accident reconstruction expert. I rarely used reconstruction experts, finding that they were easily impeached and tended to have bias for the party who paid them. The expert testified that his photo investigation of the trucks disproved my client's theory. The expert had taken several pictures of the trucks several days after they had each been towed to the junk yard. He produced several photographs that showed the left front fender of the defendant's truck was pulled out toward the front. He opined that if the defendant's truck had hit my client's truck as we contended, the fender would have been pushed in rather than pulled out.

The highway patrol had taken over a hundred photos, and I had offered only a few of them into evidence. After the defense expert testified, the court adjourned for the evening recess. We began studying all of the pictures in detail. Some pictures of the defendant's truck taken at the scene of the accident clearly showed the left front fender pushed into the left front wheel. We called and obtained the names of the wrecker crew, and visited them that evening. They specifically recalled putting a chain around the front of the defendant's truck to pull it out of the ditch. In doing so, they had pulled the fender forward from its impacted condition.

Our cross-examination the next day revealed that the expert had relied only on his own photos of the truck at the junk yard. He had not studied the highway patrol's pictures and had no knowledge that the fender had been altered by the wrecking crew.

CHAPTER III — ADVOCACY BEFORE TRIAL

The Misleading X-ray

I once defended a street railway company case in which the streetcar struck the plaintiff's vehicle from behind while the vehicle was stopped on the railcar's tracks. A number of lawsuits involved similar facts because the street car could not turn out of the way of objects on the track! The plaintiff claimed he had a hairline fracture of the leg, which was allegedly substantiated by x-rays of his leg. The plaintiff's doctor opined that the accident had caused the fracture. We took the x-ray to the railway company's physician who opined that the fracture line was almost obliterated. Although the x-ray was taken shortly after the accident, it appeared to him there were old calcium formations around the fracture. He recommended we obtain an opinion from a radiologist at the local hospital. In viewing the x-ray, the radiologist saw the plaintiff's name and observed that the name was familiar. He went to his record files and pulled out an x-ray taken four years before. It was an x-ray of the plaintiff's leg taken after a one-car automobile accident. The same linear fracture appeared only much more vividly. The radiologist stated it was clear to him that the x-ray offered in evidence by the plaintiff, taken after the street railway accident, was not a new fracture. He pointed out the calcium formations on the later x-ray which were not present on the first.

We called the radiologist to the stand. The radiologist's testimony destroyed the plaintiff's case, both because the railcar collision had not caused a fracture and because the plaintiff had denied being injured in any previous accidents.

As indicated, appearances are not always what they seem. The moral of these stories: Never take things for granted. Once the human factors enter into the picture, there is no telling what you may discover.

The Phoney Doctor

Our investigation of the facts in one case, almost proved detrimental to our client's cause in a strange way. Our client, a young business executive, was being treated by a local psychiatrist for emotional problems. The young man was finally hospitalized in the psychiatric ward of a local hospital. One day one of the nurses checked the young man's hospital chart. She noticed that "Doctor" Dale (I will call him by his assumed name because I discovered later it was fictitious as well) had just ordered the ninety-ninth insulin shock treatment for the patient. The nurse knew that this number was abnormally high (few treatments exceed thirty), so she reported it to the head of the psychiatric ward. Another doctor intervened and the young man was released. Upon his release, the young man was referred to me.

My client's story was most unusual. While he had been hospitalized, Dr. Dale advised him that his wife required counselling as well in order for the young man to have a full recovery. While the young man was still in the hospital, the doctor told him his wife was "no good" and wanted a divorce. After my client was released from the hospital, his wife called him and told him she was sorry about the divorce, but that the doctor had told her that "her husband wanted the divorce because otherwise he would never get well." He told her that it would be detrimental to the emotional well-being of her husband if she attempted to visit him in the hospital.

The two stories were so different that I asked to meet with my client's ex-wife. During that meeting, the ex-wife stated that at the divorce proceedings, Dr. Dale had testified that her husband would never recover and was totally disabled. He also testified that her husband had completely rejected her and wanted a divorce. On that basis, she obtained a default divorce. I also learned that when the young man had been originally hospitalized, Dr. Dale had told the wife that she needed consultation and treatment as well to coincide with her husband's treatment. The real kicker was that Dr. Dale's treatment of the wife occurred daily at 2:00 p.m. and these visits were nothing more than a daily seduction of the young lady. Another ironic twist in the case was that Dr. Dale was charging my client's employer for the daily sexual encounters as office visits. Because the young woman had previously had emotional problems, Dr. Dale had convinced her that these dalliances were a required part of her treatment. In fact, she had moved into the doctor's home and had lived with him for three months "as part of her needed therapy."

I filed a medical malpractice suit against the doctor. He then moved out of the state. I located him in another state and sued him there for criminal conversation and alienation of affection. When I took Dr. Dale's deposition, he testified that he had graduated from the University of Berlin in Germany in 1933. Because the school had been bombed and burned in the war, there were no records to verify his claim. He testified that he had been admitted to practice medicine in the United States in 1939, and had practiced in New York, and during the war had obtained a position with the VA Hospital.

I went to the State Medical Society. It discovered Dr. Dale had been treating heart patients as well. Strong evidence suggested that Dr. Dale had no medical degree and that he had bribed a Commissioner of the New York Medical Board to be admitted to practice in the United States in the 1930s, a practice that unfortunately occurred at that time in New York. An investigation of the hospital records revealed Dr. Dale's methods had been totally unorthodox. Indeed, the Medical Society indicated it thought Dr. Dale had learned medical terms by reading several books on psychiatry.

Based on this information, I thought it advisable to settle. I settled with the insurance company for $25,000 out of a $50,000 policy. It was not adequate, but my primary worry was that if the insurance malpractice carrier learned what I had discovered, it might void Dr. Dale's malpractice insurance. I had previously attached $12,000 of the doctor's personal funds in three bank accounts. In the meantime, Dr. Dale left the country. I obtained default judgments against him in the alienation of affection suit as well as in the criminal conversation case. I tried to enforce these judgments in Austria, where Dr. Dale then lived. But Austria would not recognize them. At least the young couple got back together and recovered some compensation for the terrible wrong done. Bizarre!

PLEADING YOUR CASE

Consider The Consequences Of What You Plead

More often than not, most lawyers give little attention to pleadings. Perhaps "notice pleading" under the Federal Rules of Civil Procedure has caused this relaxation or inattention to what is pleaded. It is often only later that lawyers realize that careless pleading has cost their client dearly. Lawyers who lose cases on judgment on the pleadings or for failure to plead a proper claim for relief or on summary judgment need only get "burned" once. Pleadings should always be evaluated in terms of all possible factual and legal consequences.

What You Plead Determines What Can Be Proven

Too many lawyers representing defendants do not view their responsive pleading, the "answer," as an important document. Too many responsive pleadings are filed by defense counsel with a "general denial." The attitude is one of total defiance to the plaintiff—"you pled it, now you prove it." By filing a general denial, counsel may be denying facts which are undisputed. Failure to admit those things that should be admitted can often open the door to opposing counsel's admission of prejudicial evidence that would otherwise be inadmissible.

General Denials Can Open Pandora's Box

Repair of property after an accident is generally inadmissible in a negligence case. The theory behind this rule of exclusion is that courts do not want to deter the landowner's repair of a defective condition; without the rule of exclusion, evidence of a later repair in a negligence action could otherwise provide an inference that the defendant would not have repaired the property unless it were originally defective as the plaintiff claimed. However, by pleading a general denial, the defendant inadvertently denies control of the property, and opens the door to proof of repair to show control over the property.

I earlier mentioned a case in which I represented an individual whose car went out of control and crossed over the center line of the highway into the path of a large milk truck. As I mentioned, no one reported the existence of a ditch, which had subsequently been filled. We filed our petition alleging negligence of the contractor, the service station, and the owner of the property. In our complaint, we alleged the control of the premises by the three defendants. Each defendant appeared separately and filed a general denial to each and every allegation in our complaint. Trial commenced. In my opening statement, I did not mention the filling of the ditch after the accident. I wanted to prove the fact before the defendants realized their mistake. As I began to prove the facts, the defendants objected. Because the defendants had denied control of the premises, the court allowed me to show the subsequent repair for purposes of showing control and for purposes of proving the existence of the ditch, which the defendants had also denied.

Do Not Plead More Than Is Necessary

One of the more humorous cases I tried focused on careless pleadings by defense counsel. I represented a woman who had fallen on a sidewalk intersecting the emergency driveway entrance into a hospital. When the hospital built the driveway some twenty years before, they had made the slope of the driveway at an almost sixty-degree angle to the sidewalk. If people were walking at night and were not aware of the sudden slope into the driveway, they were in for a real shock. When I filed the petition, we were aware that other people had fallen at the same place, but we had no names and records of these other accidents. This evidence clearly was not admissible into evidence, and we did not plead anything about prior accidents. Then the defendant's answer came to our rescue. The answer pleaded: "The driveway has been in existence for over twenty years and no one has ever previously fallen on the driveway."

We had a conference at the office: Should we move to strike the statement in the pleading? The defendant should not be able to prove this fact anymore than we had a right to plead to the contrary. We decided to extend our investigation. We conducted a house to house canvass across from the driveway, where many row houses were located. We located two homeowners who had lived in their homes for many years and both were willing to testify that several people had fallen at the driveway. Based on our findings, we decided not to move to strike the prejudicial pleading. Nor did we object when the hospital administrator testified that in twenty years "no one had ever fallen at the driveway." On rebuttal, we called our witnesses. I will never forget the little, elderly Italian lady who appeared. She said: "In the summa' time, I usta' sitta' on my fronta' porch and watcha' the people go by on the sidewalk. The people would walka' on the driveway and falla' like flies. It made me sicka' to my stomach and I no longer sitta' on my fronta' porch in the summa' time."

The moral of the story: Don't plead more than necessary.

The Evil Of Pleading Legal Conclusions

Sometimes lawyers carelessly plead legal conclusions which can be detrimental to the case. A case which best represents that lesson will always be vivid in my memory. My client owned an automobile body shop, where he would repaint trucks and tractor-trailers. Repainting was a complicated process wherein the paint was baked on the body of the vehicle in an "oven" at a very high temperature. Often, the repainting involved the body of trailers of vehicles which had hauled gasoline. In that case, it was essential that the trailer be emptied and the gasoline vapors "purged" from the trailer. Body shop personnel always directed the petroleum carrier to have the trailer purged of the vapor before delivering it to the garage for painting.

In this particular case, Phillips 66 had a tractor-trailer it wanted repainted. The gasoline company's truck superintendent told my client that it would get the trailer purged at a small local company that performed such work. When it called the small company to see if the purging had been completed, one of the employees mistakenly informed Phillips that the purging had been completed when in fact *it had not*. Phillips delivered the truck to my client. During the repainting process, the truck oven was heated to a high degree and an explosion occurred. The entire building was demolished and, most unfortunately, one of my client's employees was fatally injured in the explosion.

I represented the garage owner suing for property damage and the estate of the employee who had been killed in a lawsuit against Phillips and the small company who had allegedly purged the truck. The purging company, which had minimal liability insurance, offered to pay its insurance limits; however, Phillips refused to pay any money. Because I did not want to settle separately, the case proceeded to trial. In my petition, I pleaded that the explosion had been caused by the separate negligence of both Phillips Petroleum and the company who had failed to purge the trailer.

Both defendants denied their own negligence. Much to my surprise, however, Phillips counsel denied its own negligence and then pleaded that the negligence of the purging company was the sole cause of the accident. A careful briefing of the law revealed Phillips' error. Phillips had delivered the truck in a dangerous condition to my client. They had negligently delivered a time bomb to the garage. Its duty to deliver a purged trailer was clearly nondelegable. When Phillips admitted the negligence of the purging company, I argued that Phillips, by reason of its nondelegable duty to furnish the truck in a safe condition, had admitted its own liability. When Phillips moved for a directed verdict at the close of all of the evidence, Phillips counsel was surprised when I requested a directed verdict against both defendants on liability based upon Phillips' nondelegable duty and its admitted negligence. The judge sustained my motion.

The jury was instructed to find liability and to award my clients damages. Before the noon hour was over, Phillips counsel called and offered to pay one hundred thousand dollars for the wrongful death of my client. The property damage suit was later successfully litigated as well. As far as I am concerned, the case was won when Phillips filed its answer.

DISCOVERY

The Purpose Of Discovery

Many lawyers make a basic mistake in considering the purpose discovery procedures serve in the litigation process. They determine what they need in discovery without thinking about how they will use it. These "fishing expeditions" are perhaps more responsible for waste of time and expense during the pretrial phase of the litigation process than any other. Discovery should be calculated in the same way an attorney plans his or her order of proof in preparation for the trial. Certain basic rules should govern discovery. First and foremost, the best means of getting to know your adversary is to try to be cooperative. The new amendments to Federal Rules of Civil Procedure governing discovery are based on the general premise that all counsel should exchange material facts in as nonadversarial an atmosphere as possible. Most discovery can and should be worked out between counsel outside of court, preserving the limited resources of the court and its personnel. In my opinion, most of the lack of civility among members of the bar arises from pretrial antagonism between counsel. Each side accuses the other of bad faith long before the trial even gets underway. This approach and the resulting difficulties are stressful to the lawyers and often lead to unnecessary judicial intervention.

Working With Difficult Lawyers

Certain lawyers will always be difficult to work with. Once I called a lawyer to see if we could arrange a mutual time to take our respective clients' depositions. His response was "Serve me a notice." His client was the son of the local special agent of the FBI. The young man, who was a high school student, had been in a serious automobile accident. I told the opposing lawyer that I particularly wanted to accommodate his client because I knew the young man was attending high school. The lawyer answered: "You heard what I said: Serve me a notice." Well, I did. I served the subpoena for the young man to appear at 11:00 a.m. on a Wednesday morning. The young man arrived with counsel and with his father. I introduced myself to the father who immediately spurned me and refused to shake my hand. He then said that I was one of the most inconsiderate lawyers he had ever known because I had subpoenaed his son at a time that he was supposed to be in school attending class. I did not immediately respond. When I commenced the deposition I first read into the record the following: "Let the record show this deposition is being taken pursuant to notice duly served on counsel and subpoena served on the defendant at the time and place designed therein. The notice and subpoena in this case were necessary because counsel for the defendant refused to stipulate as to a convenient time and place for his client to appear so as to avoid the disruption of his client's classes at school. I am making this record at this time as a predicate to recover costs that were unnecessarily incurred in taking this deposition."

Opposing counsel glared at me. The father glared at opposing counsel.

Handling "The Discovery Nut"

One of the problems a lawyer faces is how to deal with the opposing counsel who for various reasons has no sense of balance or reason in engaging in unnecessary discovery. Court-imposed sanctions can deter excessive discovery, but often simply complicate matters for lawyers as well as for the court. Collateral litigation over the propriety of sanctions is too often unnecessary and excessive as well.

There are various reasons why some counsel engage in unnecessary discovery. Some lawyers simply engage in excessive discovery because they have no conceived plan or strategy. Some do it because they don't know any better. Others do not properly weigh the benefit of the discovery against its costs. Large corporations may be unaware of the excessive time their attorneys spend in needless discovery. Some corporations pay their litigation counsel through their auditing departments and the lawyer is simply paid by the invoice submitted. When it is readily apparent that a lawyer is simply running up a fee, it is difficult for the opposing lawyer to know what to do. It is wrong to follow the same wasteful process, particularly where the opposing lawyer is a sole practitioner working on a contingency fee. Of course, the lawyer can always turn to the court and seek a protective order or costs or attorney fees. But that may lead to collateral litigation and more time expended.

Two cases illustrate my point about the "discovery nut." The first was a case in which I presided as a trial judge. The assistant principal of a junior high school was a ticket taker for a professional football team. He disobeyed his employer's rule that employees could not sit in the press box during the game. He was of Italian nationality. His friend, who was a stadium supervisor, told him he would lose his job if he did not obey the rules. The employee stated he would continue to sit in the press box unless the owner of the team personally told him to leave. At this point, the supervisor, who was a friend of the principal, replied: "You better listen to me, you dumb Diego, you." The employee quit and sued the football team for discrimination based upon his nationality.

At a pretrial conference, I figured out that the actual damages could not exceed fifteen dollars a game and that the parties should therefore try to settle their differences. Defense counsel said he would be glad to pay a few hundred dollars rather than go to trial. I asked, "Then why hasn't the case been settled?" The team's counsel said that they would not pay the requested attorney fees of $20,000. It appeared that plaintiff's counsel had taken over a dozen depositions, including the owner of the team, all of the management personnel and several depositions of the players on the football team.

The case was tried, and I held that there was no intent to discriminate and dismissed the case. This holding was affirmed on appeal. No motion was made to assess costs against plaintiff's counsel for excessive discovery. If it had been made, I would have granted it. I was required to read all of the depositions. They contained no germane or relevant facts. It was obvious to me the depositions were a "fishing expedition" and totally unnecessary.

One time in an antitrust suit, I filed approximately sixty-five interrogatories seeking composite information from the corporate defendant which was located in another state. Instead of answering the questions, the opposing counsel filed over one hundred and fifty objections. Every question had multiple objections, some extending over a page in length. In total, the objections covered over thirty pages. Even formal questions were objected to in a verbose way. For example, one question was asked as to the full and formal name of the corporate defendant. The objection, as did every objection, stated that the question was "incompetent, irrelevant, and immaterial."

The case was pending in federal court in another city. I wrote the judge that I would attend court if it was necessary, but would prefer to submit the objections without argument. My adversary wrote that he wanted to orally argue his objections. I again wrote the court stating that I preferred not to attend the argument, but would do so if necessary. The court excused me. It is my understanding that opposing counsel argued each of his objections. He spent the full morning in court. A few days later the court issued a one-page order overruling all the objections.

A lawyer should not abandon his duty to defend and represent his client. However, if you are confident that excessive and unnecessary discovery is occurring, and there can be no resulting prejudice to your client, you should calculate time-saving procedures or responses to deal with counsel who are, what I call, "discovery nuts."

Calculating Discovery

Discovery, as most lawyers understand it, involves (1) depositions, (2) interrogatories, (3) admissions, and (4) production of documents or physical exhibits. In approaching discovery, I believe every lawyer should plan what evidence is needed to prove or defend their client's case and then decide by what means the evidence can be proven in trial. Normal investigative tools will reveal much of the evidence needed. By this I mean that the names of witnesses and what they know, relevant documents, photographic displays, and official reports, to name a few, can be obtained or discovered through means other than formal discovery. However, if the evidence is within the private possession or knowledge of the adverse party, then the attorney should determine what is the best means to obtain the evidence from the other side so that the evidence can be used at trial.

In utilizing the various discovery devices, counsel should be fairly certain as to what evidence he or she seeks to obtain. Thus, a basic rule is that the information you seek in discovery should already be known. Discovery procedure should serve as a tool to obtain the evidence you know exists. Fishing expeditions should be avoided.

Interrogatories

Interrogatories are especially convenient to seek the composite knowledge of a corporation. The attorney can easily request the names of witnesses having relevant knowledge of material facts. I often tell the story about a client who fell on a wet floor in a supermarket and incurred serious personal injury. We had to prove that the defendant had knowledge that the floor was wet and dangerous before out client fell. Our strategy was to use the interrogatories initially to obtain all the names of employees having relevant knowledge of the incident. The defendant company listed the name of two young clerks. We attempted to take sworn statements from these clerks, but they refused to talk to us. We took their depositions. One young man admitted that a customer had broken a bottle of liquid bleach. He had swept up the glass and without barricading the area, had left to get a mop to wipe up the liquid. He stated he was gone for about ten minutes before he returned. In the meantime, our client had slipped and fallen. She even produced her bleached skirt she had saved since the accident.

We were reluctant to call the store manager (who surprisingly claimed no knowledge of the incident until our client fell) in our case-in-chief. We also worried about calling the young store clerk for several reasons. He would obviously be "wood-shedded" by opposing counsel and we were not certain he would stand by his story. His deposition was not binding on the defendant and as an extra-judicial statement could be denied. We then drew up admissions against interest and served them on the defendant corporation. The phraseology of the admission was important—we used the exact language of the deposition:

1. Your employee found a broken bottle of Clorox bleach at approximately 2:15 p.m. on July 23 in the store aisle.

2. Your employee swept up the broken glass at approximately 2:15 p.m. on July 23.

3. Your employee thereafter left the area where the bottle broke to obtain a mop to wipe up the fluid.

4. No barricades were placed around the fluid in the store aisle while the employee went to obtain the mop.

The admissions were tendered to the managing agent of the corporation. The statements were deemed admissions against interest when not answered in ten days.

Thus, through the combination of interrogatories and depositions and admissions the crucial evidence of our case was proven at trial without the necessity of placing adverse witnesses on the stand.

Depositions

Of course depositions can be used to impeach a witness as well as to obtain admissions against interest. If an individual gives a deposition and it contains an admission against interest, it can be read into evidence. Sometimes when representing a plaintiff, a lawyer can call the defendant as a hostile witness and ask the defendant if the following questions and answers were asked when he was under oath. When doing this, lawyers should keep in mind that under discovery rules all other portions of the deposition relating to the questions asked and answers given may be read into the record as well. In taking the deposition, therefore, the attorney should be cognizant of whether a favorable admission can be obtained without having the witness testify on an unfavorable matter. On the other hand, if something might happen to a deponent before trial such that the deponent is not available at the time of trial, the deposition may then be used as evidence at trial.

Motions To Produce

A party can obtain by discovery motion pictures or physical evidence such as documents, photographs, or machinery. Once you are aware of the other side's evidence, it sometimes can be used to your advantage at trial. Using this evidence properly, whether in your case-in-chief or on cross-examination, can be an advantage. One time counsel for a plaintiff planned to prove his property damage through an appraiser and did not offer the post-accident photographs of the plaintiff's vehicle through his early witnesses. On cross-examination of the plaintiff, I requested that plaintiff's counsel produce the photographs showing the physical damage to the plaintiff's car. I argued these photographs demonstrated that the accident was the plaintiff's fault. In final argument, over much protestation from plaintiff's counsel, I argued that the jury would never have seen the photos if I had not requested them and offered them into evidence during the plaintiff's cross-examination. In other chapters I have discussed how a defendant's evidence, once discovered, can be offered by plaintiff's counsel in the latter's case-in-chief. Sometimes damaging evidence can be neutralized through such strategy.

DEMONSTRATIVE EVIDENCE

Too Much Or Too Little

As a judge, I have observed that some lawyers fail to use good judgment in the use of visual aids at trial and on appeal. Demonstrative evidence is nothing more than a teaching tool to assist the jury and the court in better understanding the evidence submitted. For this discussion, I am speaking of visual aids that are not direct evidence and that are used simply to assist in understanding the oral testimony. As so defined, demonstrative evidence is not to be confused with direct evidence, such as maps, plats, photographs, drawings, documents and other varieties of physical evidence. I assume every lawyer will utilize whatever means are available to bring direct evidence into the case.

Different judges have different rules governing the handling of demonstrative evidence. Some judges feel that such evidence should be marked as an exhibit and introduced into the record. Some judges feel demonstrative proof is not evidence at all and should not be marked as an exhibit. I think the better way to handle these exhibits is to mark them as illustrative or demonstrative exhibits and offer them into evidence for that purpose only. The lawyer should inquire how the trial judge wishes him or her to handle such evidence.

Some lawyers do not use illustrative exhibits. I think this is a mistake. Most trials include technical evidence that lay persons and often judges do not understand. Medical and engineering subjects are fields in which illustrative drawings and other means of proof (e.g. models or skeletons) are helpful. I think the expert witnesses should use their own means to illustrate their testimony. The witness then feels at ease in explaining his or her testimony to others. For example, I recommend that in interviewing a medical expert before trial, the attorney asks whether the physician has available any drawings or pictures to help the attorney understand what is going on. These same drawings and pictures can later be used by the physician witness as demonstrative evidence at trial.

Unfortunately, some attorneys can overdo illustrative evidence. These lawyers simply do not use good judgment and attempt to use drawings and transparencies to illustrate the obvious. The overuse of demonstrative evidence wastes time and annoys the judge and can offend the jury.

In one case where I sat as a trial judge, a lawyer told me he had sixty-five transparencies he wished to use in his final argument. None of them had been used in the trial. The lawyer even had the names of the parties on separated transparencies. I told him we would be in court for a week if I allowed use of these exhibits. I knew he had spent many hours and much expense in preparing the exhibits, but I felt for his sake, as well as the jury's sake, that I should exclude them and that he would be more effective without using them.

Converting The Opponent's Evidence

Demonstrative exhibits can actually contradict a witness's testimony. It is important for the attorney to explore thoroughly the use of an illustrative exhibit in light of the facts of the case so that opposing counsel cannot turn the evidence against his or her client.

In a case I earlier described, the plaintiff was injured while unloading steel beams from a gondola car. Our theory of negligence, as mentioned, was that the company employees had loaded the car with a short beam on the bottom, thus making the stack unstable. The defendant steel company cut two three-foot-long beams and brought them into the courtroom. One of the steel company's engineers showed by hand manipulations how the two beams would interlock and would not fall over even though one beam was smaller than the other. We urged that the defendant, in using the experiment, had conceded the much controverted testimony that a shorter beam was on the bottom of the stack. I called a local mechanical engineer who, with a different hand manipulation, made the beams topple. The foreman of the jury told me afterwards that our demonstration with their evidence was the convincing factor.

THE PRETRIAL CONFERENCE

Every Trial Counsel Should Insist On A Pretrial Conference

In my judgment, every case that is to be tried should have a pretrial conference with the judge who will preside over the trial. When I was trying cases, few judges in the state court held such conferences, requesting instead that the lawyers get together and agree on as many things as possible. In the federal courts today, most federal judges place the primary responsibility for the pretrial conference on the magistrate judge. Although I am aware of the time constraints of the busy trial judge, I think most trial judges should schedule conferences and pretrial conferences with the lawyers *who will actually try the case*. The fact that the trial judge pretries the case can go a long way in getting the case to settle and off the docket. Lawyers take the case much more seriously when the trial judge presides over the pretrial. Equally significant is the fact that if the case does not settle, the trial judge is intimately informed of the problems the case may present and can utilize means to make the trial more efficient and less time consuming.

The lawyers benefit from the pretrial in several ways. The lawyers can use the pretrial conference to learn as much about the other party's case as possible. The pretrial conference is the only opportunity before trial to learn what your opponent's exhibits and evidence might be. You can early appraise whether you will confront difficulties in getting certain exhibits into evidence. The pleadings should now be complete or, if they are not, this is the opportunity to learn of any amendments or surprises. What legal theories will your opponent rely upon? Counsel therefore has an excellent opportunity to appraise the strength of the adversary's case and make a vivid appraisal as to the settlement value of the case. This is true whether you are on the plaintiff's side or whether you are defending.

Most importantly, counsel can appraise the trial judge's attitude about your case. One time a lawyer had a case on the docket for over three years and each time it came up for trial he would ask for a continuance. He never intended to try it. The injury was very severe but he had not properly investigated it and had hoped the other side would offer him a settlement. However, the defendant's counsel knew what was going on and refused to offer anything but a nuisance settlement. The court finally put the case on the dismissal docket for failure to prosecute.

The lawyer came to me in desperation and asked if I would evaluate the case and try it. There was only one witness that could prove the case for the plaintiff and he lived in Chicago. He had never been interviewed. I told them I would go to Chicago and interview the witness and, depending upon what he said, I would take the case. I talked to the witness and was satisfied that I could make a case for the jury but that it would still be difficult to win. I informed the court that I was new counsel in the case and urged that the case be taken off the dismissal docket, and requested a pretrial. The court reluctantly granted my motion.

I attended the pretrial conference and immediately sensed the trial judge was disgusted with the case. It had been on the court's docket for over three years and the court let me know that if the defendant had moved for a summary judgment, he would have granted it. After the conference was completed, I turned to the judge and stated that I was fully appreciative of his attitude and that counsel who had referred the case was delinquent but that plaintiff had lost his leg in the industrial accident and deserved his day in court. I told the judge that I would never move to recuse him, but that because it was obvious that the court was frustrated about the prior handling of the case, perhaps he would feel better if he transferred the case to another judge. The next day I received an order transferring the case to another judge. I tried the case for a full week and received a fair trial, and a substantial verdict. I am confident the original judge would have directed a verdict against us. Without the pretrial and the opportunity to observe the attitude of the judge, I would have never won the case.

It is helpful for the court if the pretrial can be timed so that the trial is scheduled shortly afterwards. The pretrial conference can force lawyers to prepare briefs, proposed jury instructions, and organize their proposed evidence. Many lawyers will settle their cases rather than undergo the work required to attend the conference. In addition, the court can appraise the lawyers and the apparent factual and legal difficulties in the case. The court can then determine whether the case should or can settle.

Unfortunately, in federal courts most trial judges delegate the pretrial conference to a magistrate. Most judges feel this is more efficient, time wise, but they cheat themselves in failing to see first hand what the issues are about and whether the case can be shortened or settled. Lawyers pay more attention to the judge's observations than to a judicial officer who will not try the case.

The following anecdote illustrates the benefit of the pretrial before the trial judge who will try the case. I recently conducted a pretrial scheduling hearing in an age discrimination case where two young lawyers would hardly speak to one another. The case had been formally pretried by a magistrate who had been unable to effect a settlement. I had set the case for trial the following week. Fortunately, the plaintiff attended the pretrial conference along with counsel. It took little time to determine that the suit was more a family feud than a good faith discrimination suit. I told counsel that the defendant's offer to settle seemed very fair to me and that if the trial demonstrated what I had discerned from the pretrial conference—that plaintiff's case was not brought in good faith—I would order sanctions with costs and attorney fees against the plaintiff. I made clear to everyone that the federal court was not a forum to settle family feuds. The next day my secretary received a defiant call from the plaintiff's lawyer saying the case was settled and that he did not appreciate the judge's interference in the case.

Last but not least, a good lawyer can use the pretrial conference to overwhelm opposing counsel with preparation. Our office always carried to the pretrial conference a notebook which contained a copy of all of our exhibits, instructions, medical reports, itemized list of damages, depositions, pleadings and briefs of the law. Sometimes, to literally "scare" the other side, I had an associate bring along two other suit cases with files of other cases. In addition to having an obvious effect on counsel, the court was made well aware that we were prepared and that unless a favorable settlement was reached, the case would go to trial.

NEGOTIATION

Good lawyers must be good negotiators. If a client's interests can be satisfied without lengthy trial and appeal, the lawyer has served his client well. Knowing how to deal with one's adversaries is the key to out-of-court settlements and the negotiations that lead to that result. As the reader may well know, there are many texts and articles on the art of successful negotiation. I do not in any way wish to demean those works and the many suggested tactics prescribed for successful litigation, but every lawyer should remember what works for one person may not work for another. Equally important, it is fundamental that the facts and circumstances of a given situation demand different approaches. The different personalities of the various people involved— the parties as well as their counsel—will require varied approaches to negotiation. It should be obvious that successful negotiation between two reasonable people to resolve a disputed conflict will be pursued in a different manner than will negotiation between two or more persons where one or more is not reasonable.

In my view, two basic concepts provide the foundation for successfully negotiating a settlement. First is the old "bird in the hand" rule, i.e., that a reasonable settlement is always better than protracted litigation. The client is obviously better served under such a philosophy. Second, every situation calls for the use of common sense. This latter principle is nothing more than acting reasonably under the existing circumstances. By keeping these principles in mind, the good lawyer learns to discard unimportant concerns, such as whether an initial offer will be viewed as a sign of weakness. It is my firm belief that every lawyer, in every case, regardless of what stage of the proceedings, should try to settle the case. As every experienced trial lawyer knows, the value of a lawsuit can vary from day to day. For example, if the success of your client's case depends upon the admissibility of certain evidence and in the middle of the trial your key witness is impeached or the trial judge refuses to admit critical evidence, the value of your client's case can take a sudden turn for the worse.

Valuating Your Case

One time I represented a young businessman who lived in San Francisco. He had been in a bad accident in Nebraska. He received a severe facial scar over the right cheek. The original colored photos of the scar made his injury much worse than it was. The defendant offered $10,000 to settle. I thought the case was worth $15,000 or even $20,000. The defense then stated they wanted to take the plaintiff's deposition. I felt it worth the expense to have him fly in from San Francisco. I met him at the airport. I hardly recognized my client. He had spent the summer on the beach and was tanned like a bronze statute. He was a good looking, young man. I couldn't even see the scar. I told him: "Bill, if the other side sees you, with the liability being in doubt, I think they will withdraw the $10,000 offer. I suggest you get on the plane and go back to San Francisco." He did. I called opposing counsel and stated the client did not want to go through the deposition and would accept the $10,000.

Years ago some trial judges imposed sanctions if the parties settled a case after a set date. The idea behind the rule was to deter settlements on the courthouse steps and preserve the efficiency of the court's docket. In one case, the lawyers settled an antitrust case in the third week of trial and the trial judge fined each lawyer ten thousand dollars.

Despite the good faith purpose behind it, the rule was shortsighted. It not only deterred settlements when trial or pretrial proceedings took an unexpected twist, it overlooked that days and weeks of further trial and possible appeal could be avoided. The purpose of the litigation process is to bring satisfaction to the parties and finality to a legal dispute. It should matter little the time span in which this occurs, other than recognizing that the sooner settlements can be reached, the better the judicial process is served.

These observations are not intended to encourage courthouse set-tlements. However, the vagaries of the case and personalities of the lawyers and parties are such that not all cases can be settled before the day of trial arrives or the trial itself starts. Many defense lawyers know that certain plaintiff lawyers will never go to trial and will always settle at the last minute to avoid going to trial. Conversely, many plaintiff lawyers know that defense lawyers will often withhold their highest settlement offer until it is certain the plaintiff intends to go to trial. The better advice to lawyers is to avoid the reputation of doing one or the other.

Your Client's Case Is Unique

I was preparing to try a back injury case in which the plaintiff had had a laminectomy for a herniated disc. The plaintiff had a fairly good recovery. Back in the 1950's, this kind of case was generally valued between $20,000 or $30,000 depending on the work record and the permanency of the injury. While preparing, I read that an Oklahoma lawyer had just recovered a verdict which exceeded $200,000 in a herniated disc case. I called the lawyer to find out what medical evidence or argument he had introduced to get such a high verdict. He told me that while it was true his client had a herniated disc, the news article had omitted several important facts: the surgeon had botched up the surgery, his client had lost complete use of his left leg and could no longer work. I quickly learned that every case must stand on its own facts and it is very difficult to appraise one case by comparison with another.

The value of a case depends on the various facts peculiar to that case, including the personality of the client involved, the liability situation, the special damages that can be proven, and the gravity of the injury incurred. Lawyers on either side of litigation must honestly and objectively evaluate the case to determine its value. As plaintiff's counsel, a weak case on liability means you must discount your damages by a reasonable forecast of the percentage of your chances of winning or losing. For example, assume that you have a serious personal injury case that you reasonably calculate is worth one hundred thousand dollars if you win. If you fairly assess that the chance of losing the case on liability is greater than seventy percent, then I think it is unrealistic to request more than say $25,000 or $30,000 to settle the case. If defense counsel is unrealistic and only agrees to pay $10,000, then assuming plaintiff fully understands the risks, you have very little to lose by trying the case.

How would a reasonable lawyer negotiate under these circumstances? Either lawyer can simply say: "You know the court has asked us to try to settle the case if we can. I am certainly willing to explore the possibility if you are." Defense counsel may respond: "You have a very weak case, but I will be happy to submit whatever offer you would like to make." My response under these circumstances would be: "Look, I do not wish to argue the case with you. I think we have a good case. My client has very serious injuries and I think the jury could return a verdict into the six figure level. There are always risks in these cases on both sides. However if you are interested in settling, I will get a good faith figure from my client and submit it to you. I suggest you get a reasonable figure and we'll talk next week."

When you next meet, both sides will generally recognize that each lawyer wants to take credit for obtaining a good settlement. Usually defense counsel will be unwilling to pay the first amount plaintiff demands. Knowing this, plaintiff can try one of two tactics: inform defense counsel that the amount offered is the least that plaintiff will accept, or more realistically offer to settle for five thousand dollars more than your authorization. Plaintiffs will usually, but not always, authorize the amount their counsel will recommend. Thus, in the above hypothetical, if your goal is to try to get $30,000 for your client, a demand of $35,000 would be realistic. The higher the demand from your hoped for settlement figure, the less chance of getting a reasonable response from defendant. On the other side, defense counsel will generally offer $5,000 to $10,000 less than the amount he or she has been authorized to settle. Many defense counsel will say, "I'll give you my best shot, the maximum I am authorized." In this case, it probably will be $20,000. After this exchange, chances of splitting the difference will result in the plaintiff coming up shy of the goal of $30,000. Thus, the question becomes who has the most to lose by going to trial. If the plaintiff's counsel calculates that the chances of losing are too great, perhaps the lesser figure is more realistic to take; the converse also applies to defense counsel's appraisal. Defense counsel would hate to lose $100,000 fighting over $5,000. Sometimes plaintiff's counsel can work to compromise with hospitals and doctors if they understand their bill may never get paid (in the case of an indigent plaintiff) unless a compromise is made. Further, counsel for the plaintiff can also reduce his or her attorney fee if counsel feels it is imperative to settle.

Whatever You Do, Be Fair And Realistic

One of the problems in negotiating settlements is that often lawyers who do exclusively plaintiff's or defense work lose sight of the reasonable value of the other side's case. I recall one defense lawyer who exclusively represented insurance companies for such a long time that his attitude became that all personal injury claims were fraudulent. He tried his cases on that basis. Whenever he appeared on the other side of a case, I would not try to negotiate with him, but instead planned to go to trial. In my view, he was an unsuccessful lawyer simply because he failed to recognize the vulnerability of his own case. HE SELDOM WOULD SETTLE. His venal attitude before a jury carried little credibility; it cost his client money.

A good negotiator must gain the reputation of dealing in good faith. Remember that both you and opposing counsel have as your goal to obtain a reasonable settlement for your respective clients. Successful negotiation must be fair. Do not try to bluff a hand you do not have. Do not be afraid to try a case if appropriate. Your adversary should know that if you do not obtain a reasonable settlement, you will go to trial. One way to assure such a reputation is to prepare your cases in a thorough manner so that you are always ready to go to trial if a fair settlement cannot be reached. Having this reputation will cause other lawyers to respect you and to be more inclined to negotiate reasonably and in good faith.

Reasonable "Puffing"

There is nothing unfair in trying to get the best possible resolution for your client. Your opponent may have reasons to evaluate your case as worth more than you had thought. In that case, you can negotiate from a position of strength to obtain the best settlement possible. The following illustrates my point.

I once represented a patentee who had developed an engine shut-off device for locomotives. He had worked for Union Pacific Railroad Company, who had helped him obtain the patent. The company then arranged for him to license the patent to a small manufacturing company. The company manufactured the device and as exclusive licensee sold the device to the Electro-Motive division of General Motors, which made railroad engines. The Union Pacific in turn bought the engines from General Motors. The division had entered into an agreement with the licensee to purchase the shut-off devices when the engines were manufactured. The patentee and licensee received approximately thirty dollars per device sold as a royalty. At that time, a patent was only valid for seventeen years. Fifteen years had elapsed since the patent had been approved and, therefore, the licensee and patentee had only two more years to expect a royalty. All of a sudden, the Electro-Motive division cancelled its purchase contract and stated it was no longer interested in purchasing the shut-off device. My client went to a railroad show the next year in Chicago and found that General Motor's new engine contained his patented shut-off device. The licensee and patentee were referred to me.

My greatest concern was that the litigation would be very expensive. The largest order for any of the prior years was around two hundred devices. On that basis, the damages were less than $15,000. After several conversations with some of the officials of the Union Pacific, the licensee officials and a patent lawyer, I filed suit against General Motors for misappropriation of the patent. Rather than take the case on a contingency, I agreed to work on the case on a per diem basis. Shortly after filing suit, I received a call from General Motors General Counsel's office. The attorney indicated he would like to talk to me. Counsel flew down from Detroit and we had a friendly meeting. However, my conclusion was that General Motors had calculated the meeting as one to appraise me, whether I was the type of lawyer who would try the case, or who would simply settle for a nuisance complaint, but also wanted the meeting to try to intimidate me and my clients. The conversation was mostly one-sided; counsel informed me how much this litigation would cost, how much time a sole practitioner such as myself would have to spend on the case, and the fact that General Motors had unlimited resources to fight the case forever. I countered that my extensive investigation had lead me to believe that the defendant had misappropriated the patent and that my client's employer, the Union Pacific, was "deeply shocked" that General Motors, a company with such a great reputation, would literally steal the device without paying for it. I then informed him what he already knew—we had the benefit of a home town jury.

Counsel left without either of us mentioning the word "settlement." A week later General Motor's counsel called asking if my clients would be willing to negotiate a settlement. I said I had not discussed any dollar amount with my clients but that I would certainly convey any offers. He told me he would make one offer and if the case were not settled at that price, no further offers would be made. He then offered $75,000 to settle, an amount much greater than my appraisal of the damages. After I caught my breath and as spontaneously as possible, I stated I was certain that amount would not settle the case, but I would meet with my clients and get back to him the next day. The next day I countered with $100,000 and emphasized that my client's employer felt this was a fair price. The response was that

$90,000 was the top price along with an assignment to General Motors so it could use the shut-off device itself for the remaining life of the patent. I called back and agreed.

My conclusion: My clients were being paid an inflated value simply because General Motors was embarrassed and did not want to lose the good graces of my client's employer, the Union Pacific.

A little puffing does not hurt as long as it is used in a reasonable way and does not inhibit the desired goal.

CHAPTER IV
THE WITNESS

THE HUMAN FACTORS: THE DETERMINATION FACTOR IN EVALUATING FACTS

THE IMPORTANCE OF INTERVIEWING WITNESSES

Having A Thorough Knowledge Of What The Witness Will Say

Do Not Be A Lazy Lawyer

Always Verify Your Client's Story Before He Or She Testifies

Insist That Your Client Tell You Everything

It Is Essential To Prepare Your Witness For Trial

THE ADVERSE WITNESS

The Evil Of The Narrative Answer

The Expert Witness Is Not Always Right!

Thoroughly Check The Veracity Of All Written Documents Of An Adverse Witness

Always Treat An Adverse Witness With Respect

The Unresponsive Witness

Challenging The Credibility Of An Adverse Witness

Let The Jury Decide If The Witness Is Lying

Avoid Arguing With An Adverse Witness

PREPARING YOUR WITNESS FOR TRIAL

Make Certain To Tell Your Witnesses To Remain · Fair And Impartial When Testifying

Verify The Notes And Records of Your Witnesses

The Fire Chief's Report

Pay Close Attention To What The Witness Says In Court

CHAPTER IV — THE WITNESS

Persuading Your Potential Witness That He Or She May Be Wrong

It Does Not Hurt To Make Friends With Your Witness

Avoid Leading Questions Unless Necessary

Do Not Try to Impress the Jury With Your Erudition

THE RELUCTANT OR RECALCITRANT WITNESS

Be Polite, But Firm

A Little Psychology Goes a Long Way

*Protect Your Flanks—Don't Discount The
Personal Interest Of The Witness*

THE HUMAN FACTORS: THE DETERMINATIVE FACTOR IN EVALUATING FACTS

The difficulty with proving the truth of factual assertions of a witness is that the judge or jury will most always evaluate the testimony by the witness's personality and mannerisms. A lawyer should always remember that in the eyes of the jury, various psychological factors affect a witness's credibility. The same principle which governs all human relationships also governs here: we all tend to accept or reject other people on how we perceive them to be. A shy or timid witness may be telling the truth but the jury may well discount that witness's credibility because the witness is not able to project the testimony convincingly. Experienced lawyers will verify that even the dress or outward appearance of a witness can be a major factor in assessing credibility. Further, an unlikable witness will carry little persuasion and, may in fact, have a negative impact on the jury.

I recall a character witness in a criminal drug case. The defendant was charged with a conspiracy to distribute cocaine. The witness came to court wearing a silk suit, alligator boots and ostentatiously displayed five gold rings on his fingers. After the verdict, one of the jurors told me, "The way that one witness was dressed, we were sure he was a member of the drug conspiracy, too." In another case, police officers were accused of beating a totally innocent person in an all night cafe. The city attorney, who was defending the officers, called two women as witnesses who were obviously prostitutes. They claimed the officers did not even touch the plaintiff. When they appeared in court, they both had bleached hair, lots of make-up, and wore short, frilly dresses. The jury totally rejected their testimony.

Lawyers must be alert to the negative as well as the positive factors which will affect the credibility of their client's case. While counsel can often control dress and general appearance, it is not always possible to change the personal mannerisms of their client or the witnesses who appear on behalf of their client. As a lawyer, you have to accept people as they are. I recall a former client who was a housewife. She deserved compensation for her injuries but the jury, composed of ten women and two men, denied her damages because of her whiny voice. A jury of ten women and two men thought she over-reacted to her pain. A woman juror told me after the verdict that "one woman cannot fool ten others."

This chapter will highlight some of the problems lawyers should anticipate in handling their clients' cases, in calling witnesses, and in challenging their adversary's witnesses. The basic theme is that lawyers should prepare, prepare some more, and even then they may find themselves confronted with unpleasant surprises during the trial.

THE IMPORTANCE OF INTERVIEWING WITNESSES

The only way to plan the examination of any potential witness, whether favorable or not, is to meet and interview the witness before trial. If the opposing party or a potential witness is represented by counsel, it is, of course, unethical for counsel to conduct an interview outside of the presence of the witness's lawyer. This obstacle can be overcome by taking a deposition. Although the main purpose of discovery is to find out what the adverse party and witnesses claim to know, it is also essential that counsel appraise each witness's personality, mannerisms, and whether the witness is inclined to embellish or stretch the truth, is shy or evasive, or is perhaps overbearing and likely to alienate the jury. This personal assessment is vital for planning how to examine the witness and may well determine what questions to ask or not to ask.

The above discussion is especially relevant as it relates to the testimony of a hostile witness. Often the out-of-court informal interview can provide ammunition for cross-examination.

I was serving as defense counsel in an automobile accident case where an off-duty officer was listed as a witness on the police report. The facts of the case were highly disputed. As in many cases, the decision came down to the basic question of which party was telling the truth. The police officer was the only non-party eyewitness, so his testimony was crucial. In interviewing the officer before trial, he told me that the other side had already interviewed him and he did not wish to be further interviewed. Before agreeing to talk to me, he wanted to know how much he would be paid for his time if he appeared as our witness. It is certainly proper to offer to pay witnesses not only the minimal witness fee, but also to reimburse them for what they would lose by missing work. When informing the officer of this fact, he then told me that he was a part-time real estate salesman and felt he should be reimbursed for the time he would miss from that job if he came to court to testify. I then asked what he felt his time was worth on an hourly basis, indicating that he could perhaps be reimbursed for two hours time. He said he thought he ought to be paid for one-half of a real estate commission he might lose from a missed sale. He estimated that to be $750 to $1000. I told him that was ridiculous; that as a witness he could be subpoenaed for a nominal fee. He responded that if I did not pay him but instead subpoenaed him, he would testify that my client was at fault. At this point my interview ended.

At the trial, the plaintiff called the officer as a witness. He testified adversely to my client. Rather than cross-examine him about his testimony, which was far from the truth, I asked the officer if we had ever met before trial. I asked if he had refused to tell me what he knew. He became hostile and said, "Not really." I asked him if he did not condition his willingness to be a witness for the defense at trial on my agreement to pay him one-half of a real estate commission. He turned to the judge and said, "Do I have to answer that question?" The judge perceived what had transpired and stated firmly, "Yes, you do." He said, "I may have said something like that." I then asked, "As a matter of fact, didn't you ask for $750 to $1000 as a condition of being a witness?" He said, "I refuse to answer." After the judge directed him to answer, the officer quietly responded: "I don't recall." I asked, if the plaintiff was paying for his testimony, and he responded that he expected something. "How much?" He answered, "I don't know." "Is it $750 to $1000?" He said, "No." The credibility of the witness was destroyed—and so was the plaintiff's case.

Having A Thorough Knowledge Of
What The Witness Will Say

I have previously mentioned how foolish lawyers may look when they do not take the time to interview a prospective witness. Sometimes, however, the witness may surprise you, even when you have tried to ask the appropriate questions. I recall a humorous, but fateful incident in another automobile accident case. The plaintiff testified that my client had failed to yield the right-of-way and that my client had increased her speed as she entered an intersection. The plaintiff testified that my client told him at the scene of the accident that when she saw the plaintiff's approaching vehicle she "became excited and mistakenly put her foot on the accelerator rather than the brake." I turned to my client, at the counsel table, and quietly asked, "Did you say that to him?" She said, "Absolutely not." When my client took the stand, I asked if she had heard what the plaintiff had said about her alleged admission. I then asked her, "Did you say that to the plaintiff?" She said, "Absolutely not! I told my sister that!"

Do Not Be A Lazy Lawyer

A few years ago, I was sitting as a trial judge in a metropolitan city. The defendants were charged with robbing one of the larger downtown banks. The government prosecutor told the jury in his opening statement that he would produce several witnesses who worked at the bank to identify the two defendants. The prosecutor called his first witness, a young lady who identified herself as a bank teller who had worked for the bank for five years. The questioning proceeded as follows:

Prosecutor: You are aware that the bank was robbed on July 17?

Witness: Yes, sir.

Prosecutor: In relation to the teller window where the robbery took place, where did you work?

Witness: I worked as a teller immediately adjacent to the window where the robbery took place.

Prosecutor: Please tell the ladies and gentlemen of the jury what you observed on the day of the robbery.

Witness: I didn't see anything. I was on my lunch break and learned of the robbery when I returned.

Prosecutor: Oh, so you don't know anything about the robbery other than what you have heard?

Witness: No, sir.

Prosecutor: I have no further questions.

There was no cross-examination.

The prosecutor then proceeded to call the next witness. The witness was a middle-aged, polished gentlemen who was vice president of the bank. The questioning by the prosecutor went like this:

Prosecutor: How long have you been vice president of the bank?

Witness: Eight years.

Prosecutor: Would you please describe your duties.

Witness: (Duties described).

Prosecutor: Where is your desk?

Witness: My desk is immediately behind the teller cage which was robbed on July 17, 1981.

Prosecutor: Would you tell us what you observed at noon on that day?

Witness: I wasn't there. The month of July was my vacation and I didn't learn of the robbery until I returned from my vacation.

The jury roared with laughter.

At this point, I interrupted and requested both counsel to approach the bench. I quietly said to government's counsel: Can you tell me what is going on? He answered: "Well, judge, I never interview the witnesses. The FBI does. I am simply calling the witness list given to me by the FBI." I announced that we would take a fifteen minute recess so that the government could find out which witnesses possessed knowledge of relevant information. Failure to do so would result in personal sanctions against the prosecutor.

This same prosecutor did not fare much better when he later tried an extortion case before me. Jurisdiction can only lie under the federal statute if the conduct of the extortion "*substantially* interferes with interstate commerce." In this case, the Standard Oil Refinery had received an anonymous phone call threatening that the refinery would be blown up unless Standard Oil placed $25,000 in one hundred dollar bills in a paper sack and dropped it at a site to be designated by the caller the next day. Standard Oil called the FBI. The FBI told the oil company representatives to obtain the money as directed. However, the agents said the next day when the call came in, the FBI would make a voice print of the caller. This was done. On the second phone call, the caller directed the Standard Oil officers to throw the paper sack with the $25,000 out of a car window at a particular location at 9:00 p.m. the next evening. The Standard Oil officials were advised to come alone or a bomb would go off at the refinery. A thorough search of the refinery revealed no bomb. The next night the paper sack containing the $25,000 was thrown out of the car window as directed. As an elderly man appeared out of the bushes and picked up the sack, twenty-five agents emerged and made the arrest.

At the trial, a Standard Oil official was called as the first witness and the prosecution's problems began. As the witness told the story, the prosecutor laid foundation to play the tape recorded voice print in court. What followed was unbelievable. First, the prosecutor did not know how to run the tape player and could not get it turned on. After several minutes, this was solved and the tape began to play—only it was backwards. Finally, the tape was rewound and began to play, but instead of winding up on the receiving reel, the tape began to wind down onto the floor. The prosecutor then admitted the obvious: he had never played the tape before and did not know how to run the machine. I reluctantly granted a ten-minute recess so the prosecutor could rewind the tape.

It was clear that the prosecutor was familiar with the federal statute that the extortion must substantially interfere with interstate commerce. He had the Standard Oil official describe how he had gone to the bank, as instructed by the FBI, and had withdrawn $25,000 in one hundred dollar bills. The prosecutor then asked him, "Would you tell the jury whether or not obtaining this amount of cash substantially interfered with the business of Standard Oil?" The answer: "Heavens, no—for Standard Oil that was just a drop in the bucket!" The jury howled with laughter. The prosecutor stammered. He obviously had not interviewed the witness before trial. I tried to mitigate his embarrassment. I instructed the jury that the issue was jurisdictional and under the law the government had established, as a matter of law, substantial interference with interstate commerce.

Always Verify Your Client's Story Before He Or She Testifies

Some trial lawyers say that attorneys must always assume their clients are not telling the truth. I am not that pessimistic, but following such a rule at least makes it essential to investigate your client's version of the case. First, if you can obtain corroborating evidence of your client's testimony, it may be helpful in persuading the trier of fact that your client is telling the truth. But equally important, every lawyer should recognize the basic human characteristic of a client seeing their side of a case through rose colored glasses. It is so easy for clients to be mistaken or perhaps unknowingly exaggerate their claim or, let's face it, sometimes not to tell the truth even to their own lawyers.

Early cases taught me some hard lessons. I was defending a cement company. A young man was driving its truck which collided with the plaintiff's vehicle at an intersection. Plaintiff's counsel attempted to show that the young truck driver approached the intersection at a high rate of speed. The jury came back with a favorable verdict for my client. That evening I drove the young man home. As he left the car, he told me, "If you have time on the weekend, you should come and watch me." I said, "I don't understand—watch you where?" He said, "I race stock cars at the race track on weekends." Fortunately, the other lawyer did not know this fact either. If the insured's background had come out in the trial, it could have changed the entire case.

Insist That Your Client Tell You Everything

In another case, I represented a young man who drove a delivery truck which had been rear-ended when stopped at a stoplight. He developed a herniated disc. His doctor recommended that he change occupations so that he did not have to sit in one position most of the day. However, his physician also recommended that he pursue whatever physical activity he could tolerate. Before his deposition I cautioned him to tell everything he had done because I was fairly certain the insurance investigators had conducted a thorough study of his activities. He told me that he had gone hunting in the fall and that from time to time he had bowled in the winter. I told him it was important to disclose these facts. I asked him if there was any other physical activity he had tried and he said he didn't recall anything else. At trial, he was candid and direct about his physical activities. But I had not been thorough enough. On cross-examination he was asked if there was any other sports he had participated in. He said, "No." Then the defense lawyer marked several newspapers as exhibits. They carried the game summaries of a summer softball league. The news reports showed the plaintiff was the league's leading hitter and was selected as the catcher on the All-Star Team. At the defense lawyer's request, the plaintiff was directed to show the jury the position he had to assume in a catcher's stance. I had no basis to object. The young man said he had forgotten about playing softball. I believed him but the jury did not. The verdict was about one-half of what we expected.

An even more memorable lesson came in a case involving a young man who was a factory worker, and who had been in an auto collision. I was defending claims made against him for his insurance company. The factory worker also had a personal lawyer because he had filed a counterclaim for his own injuries. The facts of the collision were favorable to the worker. The day before the trial started, the lawyer for the factory worker asked me if I would present the case for his client on the counterclaim. We agreed it would be better if one lawyer handled the case to avoid the inference of insurance. The lawyer presented me with a resume of the insured's injuries and the claim for damages. The letter included an alleged loss of wages for six weeks following the accident. The worker testified that he had been confined to his bed for six weeks following the accident and that he had missed two months of work. On cross-examination, plaintiff's counsel simply verified what the young man had testified about his injuries and his lost time. After we rested our case, plaintiff's counsel, who was defending on the counterclaim, announced he had a rebuttal witness. Much to my surprise, the timekeeper from the worker's factory took the stand and produced time cards which reflected the insured's hours following the accident. Much to my bewilderment, the time records showed that since the accident, the defendant had worked every day, including the day of the accident. The credibility of the defendant and our case was gone. My final argument did not mention plaintiff's injuries.

These cases demonstrate that you cannot be too thorough in investigating your client's story. A client's mistake in recollection or the lack of truth can destroy his or her case. Moreover, if the client fails to tell the truth, jurors often believe that the lawyer put the client up to it.

It Is Essential To Prepare Your Witness For Trial

Many lawyers often call the interviewing of witnesses before and during trial "wood-shedding." The reader may know that in England and Scotland it is unethical for the trial counsel (barrister or advocate) to interview witnesses before putting them on the stand. I recall taking a deposition in Canada many years ago. The witness and I went over his testimony very carefully beforehand. The defendant's counsel had not interviewed the witness at all. After the trial was over, the defendant's counsel took me to lunch. He was of Scottish descent and was a very friendly person. During the course of the luncheon he turned to me and said: "I suggest ye have talked to the witness beforehand. In my country that is considered unethical." I smiled and responded and said: "I know the English rules, but the rules in the United States are different. In the United States it is unethical **not** to interview witnesses before they testify."

I have observed too many witnesses become confused on the stand and unable to articulate within the required confines of the rules of evidence what actually occurred. I recall a case in which plaintiff's counsel placed a doctor on the stand to describe surgery on the plaintiff's crushed knee. The lawyer failed to acquaint the doctor with the legal terminology required to prove a permanent injury.

The lawyer inquired: "Doctor, do you have an opinion based upon reasonable medical certainty whether plaintiff's injury is permanent?"

The doctor replied: "Only God knows that."

The lawyer was so frustrated he did not attempt to pursue the question further. The judge refused to instruct the jurors that they could award damages for permanent disability.

Perhaps our system may lend itself to lawyers suggesting testimony to witnesses or their clients (the fear of the English system), but overall, as Justice Holmes once observed, the adversary system is designed to test a witness's recollection of "truth" by vigorous cross-examination. The vast majority of lawyers possess sufficient integrity that they do not attempt to tell the witness what to say. Most lawyers interview witnesses to make certain they can accurately relate relevant testimony. Without earlier recorded statements to refresh a witness's memory, it is difficult for any witness to recall events which have taken place months and sometimes years ago. If a witness is not telling his version of an incident according to his own knowledge or observation it can more often than not be brought to light on cross-examination.

THE ADVERSE WITNESS

The Evil Of The Narrative Answer

In product liability trials, expert witnesses are often necessary. In a case in which I represented the plaintiff, the Chief Engineer of the defendant manufacturer was a well-educated individual. Being from Brooklyn, he had an accent that was distinctively not from the Midwest. He possessed one characteristic which often haunts professional witnesses—he liked to hear himself talk. His answers were never short and to the point. Rather, each answer contained long narratives, prefaced by "let me explain." At the beginning of his testimony, I objected on grounds that the answer was either not responsive or, in fact, was a narrative answer. Each time I objected, the court enthusiastically, it seemed, sustained my objection. But when the witness continued to belabor his answers with long, erudite and technical statements, I perceived that I was not the only one irritated by his answers. Not only could I tell that the trial judge was annoyed, but I sensed that the jury was becoming irritated as well. I then ceased objecting and let the witness continue to provide his irritating and boring responses. Opposing counsel was oblivious to what was going on. He allowed the witness to ramble on and on and on. The witness was on the stand for his direct examination from Thursday morning into Friday afternoon.

As the examination progressed, it became readily apparent that the court reporter was extremely irritated by the witness's long answers. After all, the longer the answers, the more the reporter must record. At that time, the reporter was still using shorthand to record the proceedings rather than the current stenotype machine. Finally, at about 3:15 on Friday afternoon, while the witness was in the middle of a long answer, the trial judge interrupted and said: "Mr. Witness, it has been a long week and I promised Mr. Brown, our court reporter, that we would adjourn early today at 3:00 p.m. It is now 3:15. How much longer will it take you to finish your answer?"

I'll never forget what happened next. The witness looked at his watch and said: "Oh, I think I can finish in another fifteen minutes." Just then I saw a black projectile float in front of me. The court reporter had thrown his fountain pen across the room and said, "Brother, you are through right now!" The jury roared. The judge smiled and much to everyone's relief, announced: "Ladies and Gentlemen, I guess we are adjourned. Have a nice weekend." The jury roared again.

We were one up on gamesmanship!

The Expert Witness Is Not Always Right!

One of the more interesting cases I encountered in my trial practice involved a road contractor sued by a large oil company for an unpaid fuel bill. I represented the road contractor. In the course of building a highway, my client's earth moving equipment developed motor trouble and performed poorly. He soon fell behind his schedule. Eventually, many of his dirt movers and other diesel machinery became inoperative. He traced the problem to the fuel he was using and made inquiries of the oil company representatives about whether the diesel fuel met the standards necessary for proper performance. The company that had sold him the fuel represented it had tested the fuel and that it met industry standards required of performance for diesel machinery. In desperation, the contractor decided to switch from diesel fuel to kerosene. The kerosene contained no impurities, but it was much more expensive, and consequently the project was more costly than antici- pated. Nonetheless, the contractor determined that using kerosene was the only way to cut down on penalties he was incurring in failing to complete the job on time.

When the contractor refused to pay $10,000 for the fuel, the oil company sued him. Fortunately, the contractor had saved some of the fuel he had used and removed from the diesel equipment. I sent the fuel samples away to a testing laboratory in Fort Worth, Texas. The report came back that both the sulphur and carbon content of the diesel fuel exceeded the maximum levels under industry standards. The testing laboratory supported our theory that the diesel fuel sold by the oil company was of poor quality. On this basis, we counterclaimed for $200,000 against the oil company. We proceeded to trial in the federal district court.

The trial lasted more than six weeks. The testimony of our testing laboratory fuel experts went fairly well. On rebuttal, the oil company urged that the testing done by our experts was inaccurate and that its experts and their tests would disprove our theory of the case. One of their experts did indeed change the course of the trial, but not in the way the oil company hoped.

At first, the oil company's expert witness appeared to swing the momentum of the trial against us. He was a chemical engineer at one of the oil company's large refineries in Oklahoma. He was likeable, very professional, and, I might add, believable. He had conducted an ex- periment which he stated "proved conclusively" that the tests con- ducted by the Fort Worth laboratory were inaccurate. He said his tests conclusively established that the fuel sold to our client did not contain impurities *when sold*.

The engineer related that the contractor had taken his fuel samples from the diesel machinery at the job site during the summer. Before having the samples tested, the contractor had placed the fuel (which was black and dirty in appearance) in glass jars and had sealed them with screwed-on caps. The oil company expert testified that the con- tractor had placed the jars in the window of his tool shed where they were exposed to the hot summer sun. The engineer explained that the "actinic rays of the sun had penetrated the glass jars and had caused the molecular composition of the hydrocarbons within the fuel to change." This chemical process had increased the carbon content of the oil such that when tested, the fuel contained an unusually high level of hydrocarbon.

The witness testified that an experiment he had conducted verified the accuracy of his opinion. He had obtained samples of the same diesel fuel sold to the contractor and placed a gallon of the fuel into two glass jars. The fuel was clear when obtained from the refinery. He brought the two exhibits with him. He had placed the first jar in a dark closet and left it sealed for six weeks. After six weeks, this fuel was still clear and contained no evidence of impurities. The remaining fuel was placed in another glass jar in an open field for six weeks during the summer. The engineer tested the temperature level of the fuel every day by opening the top of the jar and measuring the temperature. The oil had averaged over 100 Fahrenheit because of the hot sun. The fuel in that jar was black as night. Based on this test, the engineer testified that the actinic rays of the sun had caused the change in the molecular composition of the fuel in the jar left in the sun. He concluded that the same actinic rays had changed the contractor's sample of fuel, and this chemical process caused the impurities. By contrast, the sample the engineer had placed in the dark closet had remained clear.

The oil company rested their direct examination at the end of the day. Court was adjourned. Cross-examination was to convene in the morning. I don't think I have ever left a courtroom feeling more depressed. We immediately called the scientists at the Fort Worth testing lab and explained how the oil company engineer had refuted our entire case. At 3:30 a.m. that morning the telephone in my hotel room rang. An engineer in Fort Worth said "This is so simple I can't believe I missed it." He told me to obtain a copy of *Webster's Dictionary* as well as the latest edition of *The Handbook on Chemistry and Physics*, available at any library. They state that actinic rays of the sun are ultra violet rays and cannot penetrate glass. An early call that morning to the local university obtained the services of a chemical engineer. We met for breakfast. He agreed that the reason the oil company sample placed in the field changed composition and the sample in the closet was clear was not because of the rays of the sun, but because the sample in the field was tested daily for temperature. In doing so, the company engineer had unwittingly allowed oxygen into the sample everyday. The fuel sample had oxidized for six weeks, producing impurities.

At court that morning, our cross-examination of the oil company engineer seemed to support his testimony from the day before. I merely asked him to repeat how the jar had been opened each and every day to allow for an accurate temperature reading. We did nothing more than allow the company's expert to confirm his direct testimony emphasizing the inaccuracy of our own tests and repeating how his test conclusively proved that the contractor had preserved inaccurate samples by placing his samples in the window where the actinic rays of the sun had done their job.

I then called the university professor as our rebuttal expert witness. I questioned him concerning *Webster's Dictionary* and the latest edition of *The Handbook of Chemistry and Physics.* Both texts with proper foundation as laid by the university professor qualified for admission into evidence. The professor read portions from each work about the actinic rays of the sun. Each work verified that actinic rays of the sun are ultraviolet rays which cannot penetrate glass. The university professor pointed out how one does not become sunburned through a car window because the ultraviolet rays of the sun do not penetrate the window glass.

After the university professor's testimony, we rested. The judge then announced the noon recess. He said, "When we return, I am sure that the oil company will present their rebuttal." After lunch, counsel for the oil company stood up and announced that they rested and had no further rebuttal.

The jury returned a substantial verdict for my client. The moral of the story: expert witnesses can be wrong and can fool themselves.

Thoroughly Check The Veracity Of All
Written Documents Of An Adverse Witness

Sometimes, merely reviewing the doctor's notes is not enough. In one case I worked on, a pediatrician was treating a newly born baby for tetany, a nervous condition that causes infants to shake or tremble. To treat the condition, the doctor prescribed a drug which should be given orally or intravenously (IV). On the hospital record, the doctor mistakenly wrote that the drug be given intramuscular (IM). Although the instructions on the drug vial read "DO NOT GIVE INTRAMUSCULAR," the nurse felt that the doctor's orders overruled the directions on the vial. The infant was given the drug by needle into the muscle, and the child eventually lost use of that leg. Unbelievably, when the doctor found out about his error, he erased the order so that it stated that the drug should be given orally or by intravenous injection. He blamed the nurse for misreading his order.

The nurse told me that the hospital record had been changed. We submitted the record to a handwriting expert. When the record was placed under an ultraviolet light, the original, erroneous order was visible, and the expert concluded that the report had been changed. We thoroughly impeached the doctor in his deposition and the case was settled.

In the FELA case mentioned in the previous chapter, the plaintiff had injured his back lifting telephone poles to repair a phone line along the railroad tracks. I wanted to prove that the plaintiff was a good and regular worker before he was injured. I subpoenaed the work sheets he had filed each day. There were hundreds of them, one for every day he worked for the railroad showing the work he had completed each day. Upon inspecting each of the sheets, I was astonished to find one report written over a year before his injury which was signed by the plaintiff and read, "I fell off the top of the pole today and I am going to sue the f_____ railroad for a million dollars." I confronted my client and asked if he had written the report. His answer was—"I sure don't remember the incident, but I could have written it. It looks like my handwriting, but I'm not sure." I decided to have a handwriting expert examine the report. Much to my relief, the expert stated that my client's signature had been traced and the rest of the report was not in his handwriting. I decided to confront the railroad's lawyer to see if the railroad was trying to surprise us with the report during the trial. The railroad's lawyer was honorable; however, from prior experience, I believed the railroad's claim adjustor was not.

The railroad's counsel reported that he was unaware of the report but that the claim adjustor told him he wrote it as a "joke" to scare the railroad's supervisor. I told counsel I wanted to put the adjuster on the stand. He moved the trial court to suppress the report. The law was clear I could not call the adjuster as a witness for purposes of impeaching him. However, under the circumstances, the law does consider the admission of a false report as an admission of liability. On that basis, the judge allowed me to show the whole incident. I was glad I had taken the time to inspect each one of the work reports.

Always Treat An Adverse Witness With Respect

It is natural for any lawyer to become irritated when confronted with a biased witness for the other side. Even if adverse witnesses are not telling the truth, the opposing counsel should never call them liars or rogues. One time in a suit against a bus company, I called two

THE ADVERSE WITNESS

women passengers as witnesses. The plaintiff's lawyer, who had tried many criminal cases, made the fatal mistake in final argument by saying to the jury "You can't believe those two floozies the bus company called as witnesses." A jury may easily take the witness's side and silently condemn the lawyer if they feel counsel is not being fair or is being argumentative with a witness. Jurors often relate to the lay witness and interpret a lawyer's arguing with a witness as an effort by counsel to exercise superiority over someone, who like the jury, is not trained in the law.

The Unresponsive Witness

What then should an attorney do when confronted by a witness who either refuses to provide a responsive answer to a question or tries to embellish a response with unresponsive conclusions? Counsel must protect the record and control the examination, but keep in mind that the lay jury can become impatient with lawyers who continually cut off the witness's response and do not allow the witness to make a complete answer. I have observed lawyers who interrupt the witness with the words "just answer the question 'yes' or 'no.'" Some lawyers interrupt and move to strike a witness's answer when in fact the witness is simply trying to respond to the question completely. The jury may sense that counsel was unfair to the witness when the judge states, "Overruled, the answer will stand." Sometimes a trial judge will interrupt the witness with a request to confine an answer to the question asked. But when the court does not and counsel finds the witness's answers are unresponsive, it is often prudent to interrupt and politely say something like this to the witness: "I appreciate your desire to comment on other matters, but I will cover them in later questions. If I do not, I am sure your lawyer will ask you further questions if necessary. I don't mean to cut you off, but we will all be able to move along more quickly if you try to confine your answers to the questions asked."

The point is, it is better not to risk alienating the jury. If you continue to have problems with the non-responsive witness, you may need to politely turn to the court and simply say: "Your Honor, I move to strike the answer as not responsive and I would respectfully ask the court to please instruct the witness to simply answer the questions asked." When you are certain you are right, this approach usually will work.

CHAPTER IV — THE WITNESS

Challenging The Credibility Of An Adverse Witness

Sometimes, there are more effective ways to show a witness is mistaken than by attacking their credibility on cross-examination. One time a seventeen year old woman was a witness to an accident that occurred at a farm driveway off of a major highway. She was waiting at the east window of her farm house for a ride from a neighboring farmer. My client was a passenger in a car, which had rear-ended the farmer's automobile before beginning to turn into the driveway. My client testified that the driver of the car in front had suddenly slowed down and then, without warning, stopped abruptly on the highway before turning into the driveway. The issue was whether the farmer had signaled that he was going to turn off the highway.

The farmer who was driving the first car testified that he had not seen my client's car approaching from the rear, but that he had gradually slowed to turn into the driveway and had signaled with his turn signal for a reasonable distance. My client and the driver of the second car testified that the driver of the first car had not signaled a turn. The young lady who was waiting for her ride was called as a witness for the farmer and testified rather convincingly that she had seen the cars approach and that the neighboring farmer in the first car had clearly signaled his turn into her driveway.

Much to the satisfaction of my opposing counsel, and to the surprise of the jury, I rested without cross-examination. I did not want to risk embarrassing the girl in front of the jury by even suggesting she was not telling the truth. On rebuttal, I recalled a highway patrolman, an engineer and a photographer. The highway patrolman identified the point of impact as fifty feet west of the driveway. The engineer testified that he accompanied me before trial to the young lady's farm house and that I had identified myself to her parents as a lawyer in the forthcoming case. He explained that the parents had given us permission to take some pictures from the window of the farm house where their daughter was waiting for her ride. The window was located at the rear of an "L-shaped" porch and the house projected out fifty feet to the south of the west side of the window. We discovered that the house completely blocked the view of the approaching car, the young lady's view of the turn signals, and the approach of either car. The engineer demonstrated how the young woman's view was obstructed by using drawings done to scale. The photographer took pictures illustrating the line of sight. The young lady, out of friendship, was obviously *mistaken.* She could not have seen the vehicles prior to impact. However, if I would have questioned her veracity after her direct examination, I would have risked angering the jury. We avoided that confrontation, and yet were able to show she had not told the truth.

Let The Jury Decide If The Witness Is Lying

Attorneys should remember that jurors know when a witness is not being truthful. In a breach of contract case, an accountant for the company my client sued produced a balance sheet on his direct examination that showed my client, a franchisee, had a $300,000 deficit in his account. Before trial, I had discovered that the company's balance sheet contained a mathematical error that accounted for the deficit. As I began to cross-examine the company's accountant concerning the error, we came to a recess. Upon returning to the court, I picked up the balance sheet and resumed my examination. I asked if the balance on the sheet was incorrect and whether the company had relied on a mistaken balance sheet in terminating my client's franchise. The accountant then made his first mistake. He said the balance sheet was correct. As I began to approach him with the sheet, I noticed that the original figure on the exhibit which I had showed him earlier that morning had been erased and the correct balance was now shown. I asked him if he had altered the sheet at recess. He then made his second and more fatal mistake. He answered "no." I reminded him that he was under oath and that if necessary, I could bring in a handwriting expert to show that the sheet had been altered. The accountant then admitted that he had erased the sheet at recess, but said he did so because the mistake was obvious and he wanted to correct it. However, by changing the balance sheet, his testimony conflicted with the deposition testimony of several company officials who had claimed that my client had been discharged because his account was in arrears over $300,000.

In final argument, I asked the jury to evaluate all of the testimony and particularly the accountant's testimony and conduct in deciding which side was telling the truth. The truth, as the jury found, was that the client had built up a large trade territory and the company had decided it was profitable to terminate the franchise and take it over themselves.

CHAPTER IV — THE WITNESS

Avoid Arguing With An Adverse Witness

Arguing with an adverse witness doesn't pay off! When I started practicing law, one of my early cases was a will contest between brothers in a large family. The testatrix, the matriarch of the family, had left her large estate solely to one brother and his wife, who had lived with the testatrix the ten years preceding her death. The matriarch had turned senile the last year and our clients, two other brothers, claimed that the third brother and his wife had unduly influenced her to execute her last will at a time when she was not of sound mind.

An old family physician had treated the testatrix all her life. The lawyer for the estate had subpoenaed him to give a deposition. Our goal was to obtain the doctor's testimony that the testatrix was not of sound mind when she had executed her last will and testament. The doctor had previously provided both sides a report that the testatrix was senile at the time during the last year of her life. Before the deposition, I visited with the doctor. At the conclusion of my visit, I told the doctor, "I must tell you we have a weak case because we have found out that five years before she died, she had executed almost an identical will leaving the bulk of her estate to the same son and daughter-in-law." The doctor said, "Well, I would like to help you because this one son and his wife took advantage of my patient most of her life, but I can verify only that she was actually senile during the last two years of her life. So don't ask me about the earlier time because I could not give the same opinion about her mental status beyond the last two years." I told him, "Well, we will handle one problem at a time. Our main goal now is to set aside the will that has been filed for probate. I won't ask you about her condition at the time of the first will."

The time came for the deposition, which was held in the doctor's rather small office. The lawyer for the estate was an experienced, able trial lawyer but he was also highly excitable, impatient, and easily irritated. I had observed in past cases with him that he sometimes "lost his cool" and irritation often turned to anger—and it showed.

THE ADVERSE WITNESS

During the course of the deposition, the opposing lawyer became irritated with the good doctor's testimony that the testatrix lacked a sound mind on the date she executed her last will and testament. I can vividly reconstruct what ensued during the opposing lawyer's cross-examination:

Q: Doctor, I notice you are testifying without any notes or records.

A: Yes, sir.

Q: How can you remember all of the events and the condition of your patient without notes?

A: I treated her all my life. In the past two years I saw her two or three times a week—sometimes in the office, sometimes at her home.

Q: Did you make records of her visits and her condition?

A: I am sure I did.

Q: Will you produce the notes for me to look at?

A: No.

Q: Why not?

A: I don't have them here.

Q: Where are they?

A: At my house in the attic.

Q: Will you get them?

A: No.

Q: Why not?

A: Because I don't need them to tell you of her condition and I do not have time to look for them.

As the questioning continued, the voices of the opposing counsel and the doctor rose in volume.

Q: Can you have a member of your staff look for your records?

A: I could have my son and daughter look for them.

Q: Would you do that?

A: Not unless you pay them for their time.

Q: How long would it take?

A: Weeks. All my old records are scattered together in several trunks in my attic.

Q: How much would it cost?

A: Well, my son and daughter are busy people, but I suppose they would do this for about $50 an hour, a piece.

Counsel said "That is ridiculous."

A knock on the door. A nurse opened the door and said, "Doctor, all the patients can hear you folks yell."

Our adversary, very irritated said, "I have just a few more questions," again in a loud and angry voice:

Q: Doctor, are you aware that five years before she died she executed an earlier will?

A: I am told she did.

Q: What is your opinion as to the mental capacity of your patient at that time?

A: She was crazy as a loon then, too!

The doctor had become so irritated at counsel, he lashed out against him. I don't know who would have won the credibility argument in front of the jury. We never had to find out. The doctor's testimony influenced the other side to make a substantial and fair settlement.

PREPARING YOUR WITNESS FOR TRIAL

Make Certain To Tell Your Witnesses To Remain Fair And Impartial When Testifying

This admonition may seem contradicted by the incident just related. In the above incident, I think an impartial factfinder might have doubted the credibility of the doctor. My experience is that jurors often discredit a witness who becomes argumentative and biased on the witness stand.

One time, in defending the railway company, I was confronted with a physician who attempted to exaggerate the seriousness of the plaintiff's injury. He claimed that when hit by a street car, the plaintiff had broken the navicular bone in his wrist. I had the plaintiff examined by a physician who told me that he could find no evidence of fracture on the x-rays. He produced two orthopedic books which showed that it was essential to keep a cast on a broken navicular bone for eight weeks in order to keep the bone immobile. The medical texts stated the navicular bone is a small bone in the wrist which receives very poor blood circulation, so that failure to keep it immobilized could cause necrosis (the bone will not heal) to set in. The physician had not placed the wrist in the necessary cast. He had simply furnished the plaintiff a sling. I asked the doctor on cross-examination whether in the case of a navicular bone fracture it was essential to cast the wrist to keep the navicular bone immobile. He agreed with the orthopedic text books I produced. Hoping to help the plaintiff, he stated the reason he had not placed a cast on the plaintiff was that plaintiff was such a poor man that he couldn't afford to pay the doctor for a cast! We won the case. Afterwards, two jurors sought me out and said all members of the jury had agreed that they wouldn't hire the plaintiff's doctor to treat their dog!

The Corollary To The Above Axiom:
When You "Woodshed" Your Witnesses
Before Trial, Remind Them That Whatever
Happens On The Stand, They Must Tell The TRUTH.

Some accident victims try to conceal prior accidents on the theory that the other side will not find out about them. This almost always backfires. Counsel should advise their clients that they should assume that the other side will always know more about them than they themselves remember. As I have earlier observed, it is the lawyer's duty to talk to the client and to the material witnesses. Obviously, you cannot tell witnesses what they should say. The witnesses must testify only about what they know. They must not refuse to disclose the truth when they are asked to do so. Failure to do so can only mean trouble.

I have known clients who have tried to conceal prior injuries from their own treating doctor. This can lead to obvious embarrassment and impeachment of the physician as well as the client.

I once tried a wrongful death case in federal court in St. Louis, Missouri. I represented the estate of an individual worker who had been killed while working at a steel foundry using a grinding wheel. I recovered the broken wheel which had hit the decedent on the forehead. My problem was finding an expert witness who could tell me about proper bonding and manufacturing of the wheel. In my research, I discovered that the grinding wheel industry, at least at that time, had no satisfactory means to test the wheel under stress. All the tests were directed to a free running wheel. Unfortunately, every knowledgeable expert I could find worked for the grinding wheel industry. I determined that every manufacturer of grinding wheels was a member of the Grinding Wheel Institute. Understandably, no one who worked for the Institute would agree to testify against any company member of the Institute. I then researched the few cases that had been tried and reported and called the lawyers who had represented plaintiffs in those cases. I found that several had used a common expert. His name was Tom McSweeney, a material engineer who taught at MIT in Boston.

I visited MIT and was very impressed with McSweeney's professional background. After all, he was on the faculty of one of America's prestigious engineering schools. He convinced me that the manufacturer's testing had been deficient. Of course, as plaintiff's counsel, I was easy to convince.

The trial was scheduled in St. Louis in February 1958. I wanted McSweeney to be there when I picked the jury and to hear my opening statement. It also gave me a chance to review his testimony and to go over with him the defense's theory so I could better prepare him for cross-examination. The night before he took the stand, we ate dinner together and I went through his professional background. One thing of which he was proud was that he had worked as a consultant for various companies on research projects connected with the United States Government's national defense program during World War II. He stated he was not at liberty to disclose the details of those research projects. I told him simply to mention the work as part of his background without going into detail. I also asked about his background with grinding wheels. He stated that although he had never been employed by the industry, he was quite familiar with the manufacturing process because he had observed the process in nine different manufacturing plants. I, of course, thought this important. When I asked him on what occasions he had visited the various Carborundum plants, he stated that he had testified as an expert witness for plaintiffs in six different cases and had been retained to be an expert witness in several others. I advised him that if this were to come out in the testimony, the defense lawyer will likely portray him as a professional witness for plaintiff attorneys, which would detract from his credibility and professional objectivity. I said, "Let's not bring that out."

Our conversation almost led to disaster. McSweeney took the stand. He was an old Irishman. Fortunately, so was the judge. During some breaks in McSweeney's one-and-a-half days of testimony, before and after recess, the judge slid his chair over to the end of the bench and visited with McSweeney. It was obvious that the judge liked McSweeney. As cross-examination began, the defense counsel asked:

Q: Mr. McSweeney, have you ever been inside the plant of any grinding wheel manufacturer to observe the manufacturing process?

A: Yes, I have.

Q: How many?

A: As I recall, approximately nine.

Counsel then took out the list of manufacturing companies, which numbered, as I recall, over twenty-five, all of which belonged to the Grinding Wheel Institute. Counsel started at the top.

Q: Have you ever been in the Bethlehem plant at Bethlehem, Pennsylvania?

McSweeney looked at me and responded: "I cannot answer that question on the ground it is confidential information."

Defense Counsel: Have you ever been in the Carbordum Company in New Jersey?

McSweeney: I cannot answer that question because that is confidential information.

Defense Counsel: Your Honor, I would request the court to direct the witness to answer.

Before we hit rock bottom, I thought I would try to salvage it. I interrupted and said, "Your Honor, I don't know what the problem is, but if I could approach the witness, perhaps I could find out." The Judge responded, "Good idea."

I stepped forward to the witness chair and whispered to McSweeney, "Tom, What is going on?" He said, "Well, you told me not to bring up the fact that I had been in those plants for those plaintiff attorneys." I said, "Tom, you have to answer if the other side asks the question. If you don't, watch out or we'll both be in jail."

As I returned to my seat, I took a calculated risk. I stated, "Your Honor. Mr. McSweeney states he can reveal which manufacturing plants he has been in, but prefers he not be asked about the purpose of his visit." The Judge agreed, "That's a good idea." He said, "It was probably confidential work for the United States Government and he, therefore, should not have to reveal the name of the client."

CHAPTER IV — THE WITNESS

Much to my great relief, defense counsel settled for McSweeney's limited answer. I have often looked back on that experience and thought how foolish I was not to reiterate to the expert his obligation to tell the truth if asked. I think that is the closest I came to being held in contempt of court. I probably should have been.

Verify The Notes And Records Of Your Witnesses

Sometimes, doctor's notes, hospital records or work records will contain irrelevant opinions or harmful statements. Counsel must be aware of such opinions or statements before trial. It is too late when these opinions and statements are revealed in records as an exhibit at trial. I remember a case where my client, the plaintiff, had been severely injured but became a problem patient for his treating physician. His doctor reached a point where he simply did not like this patient. The defendant wanted to take the doctor's pre-trial deposition. The doctor had written a thorough report which I had produced for inspection. I interviewed the doctor before the deposition. I asked if I could see his office notes. During one of the patient's visits, the doctor had written in his records: "The patient visited today and said if I didn't send a strong report about his injuries to the insurance company, he was going to hire a crooked doctor and a crooked lawyer and sue for a million dollars." I said, "Doctor, why would you write such a note in your report?" He said, "I don't know. At the time I was thoroughly disgusted with the patient and he yelled this to me as he went out the door." Once again, a lawyer must deal with the records which exist. For one thing, I did not want to appear to be a "crooked" lawyer. I asked the doctor if he could testify from his written report without reference to the notes. He said he could. However, I reminded him if the other side asked him for his offices notes in the deposition (something every lawyer should do) he must produce them. Once again, I was greatly relieved when defense counsel did not request the doctor's office notes.

The Fire Chief's Report

In a gas explosion case, we claimed that the gas company had negligently failed to cap the main valve to an open line at the same time its employee attempted to light a newly installed water heater. I represented the owner of the building. We called the Fire Chief as a witness in our case. The Chief had been with the fire department for many years and was quite a character. He testified that he observed the gas meter dial going around after the explosion, indicating gas was still coming into the demolished building. When the gas company presented its case, the defense counsel produced a handwriting expert who testified that the Fire Chief's report had been erased and that the original typewritten report read that no gas was flowing through the meter when he had arrived. Our whole case was based on the gas being negligently turned on into an open pipe. On rebuttal, we called the Chief to return to court and explain why he had changed the report. He stated that his assistant had prepared the report and had not seen the meter that the Fire Chief had observed. The Fire Chief had to sign the report and therefore he corrected it to reflect the truth.

It would have been much better if we had discovered this fact before the Chief had testified. My lack of thoroughness and total reliance on an official document allowed an issue of credibility to come unnecessarily into the case.

Pay Close Attention To What The Witness Says In Court

When you are questioning a witness, and anticipating what you think the answer will be, sometimes you think ahead and do not pay close attention to what the witness has actually said. Lawyer's need to guard against this habit and pay close attention to the answer. In the case with the Fire Chief that I just related, I asked the Chief what he observed when he arrived at the explosion site. He answered, "The meter dial was moving around at about the speed of the *minute hand* on my watch." I assumed that he said the "second hand" on the watch. Counsel for the gas company carefully avoided this testimony on cross. He obviously planned to argue the point to the jury when it would be too late to explain. He did not want the Chief to have an opportunity to explain.

Later, as I was using a hypothetical question with my expert witness to prove that the explosion had been caused by gas entering the building, I asked my chemical engineer to assume there was evidence that after the explosion gas was still entering the building as evidenced from the fact that the Fire Chief had observed the meter dial going around at the speed of the *"second hand"* of the watch. Defense counsel objected to my question, and the judge sustained the objection. The judge pointed out that the Fire Chief had not said the *second hand*. I said, in front of the jury, "I don't think that's right, Judge. The movement of the minute hand on the watch would be difficult to observe." Defense counsel jumped up and said, "That's just the point."

I checked the record. Counsel and the judge were correct. I asked permission to recall the Chief to clarify his answer. Over vigorous objection, the court allowed me to recall the Chief. I rushed out to the Chief's home and he told me that he had testified correctly because he always called the hand of a watch which moved around in one minute, "the minute hand." I was very relieved, but then I said, "What do you call the hand that points to the minutes?" He stated that was "the hour hand." Relaxed, I asked the Chief to reappear to clarify his answer so that I could recall my expert witness and go forward with my hypothetical question.

The Chief appeared and took the stand, testifying as he had told me the night before. On cross, defense counsel boldly questioned the Chief as follows: "So, you call the hand that shows the seconds a minute hand?" The Chief responded, "Yes, sir." "You say the hand that shows the minutes, is the hour hand?" "Yes, sir," said the Chief. Then counsel defiantly approached the witness and questioned, "Well, if that's true, what do you call the hand that points to the hour?" I blinked and thought to myself, "The Chief is trapped." But the Chief spontaneously replied, "The twelve hour hand." The jury roared.

Saved by the bell again!

Persuading Your Potential Witness
That He Or She May Be Wrong

Witness's recollections can often be mistaken. When a witness does remember incorrectly, attorneys should use every effort to convince the witness of his or her mistake. Official reports or documents can sometimes demonstrate to witnesses that their testimony may be mistaken. Professional journals can also help. I once had a case in which I represented a young girl who had lost her right kidney after being thrown from a horse she had rented at a livery stable. Her surgeon was reluctant to say that the young lady had any permanent disability. "She can function just as well with one kidney." Obviously, the injury was permanent, since she had lost one of her two kidneys. I pointed out that if she incurred any infection or injury to the second kidney, she could very well die. He agreed. Yet, he refused to change his opinion. This opinion seemed to me short-sighted and minimized the full extent of the plaintiff's injuries.

I went to the University Medical Library and researched the effects of the loss of kidney. I found one topical article entitled "Disability For Loss of Kidney," which appeared in a German medical journal. I copied the article and hired a German professor at the University to translate the article into English. The article stated that in Germany at that time an individual who had lost a kidney was given a 20% permanent disability rating under a state pension system. I showed the article to the surgeon. He said, "Well if that's what they do in Germany, we can do it here as well." His testimony at trial—the plaintiff had a 20% permanent disability.

It Does Not Hurt To Make Friends With Your Witness

In a major case where the plaintiff's injuries were quite severe, our best witness, a rural sheriff, was potentially the most damaging witness as well. Our client, a Texas resident, was visiting in rural Nebraska. While traveling on a state highway, he turned off the highway into a small town to buy gasoline. If he had continued another quarter of a mile, he would have found a detour on the state highway caused by road repairs. However, when he left the town filling station, he was directed back to the state highway on another road just outside the small town but beyond the point of the detour. However, the road was still open to local traffic. The road contractor had failed to put up barricades on that road, so no warning signs were posted. It was at dusk and visibility was not optimal. Our client proceeded down a hill at a speed of 55 to 60 miles per hour. As he neared the bottom of the hill and began to go up the next hill, he ran into a large piece of road machinery, which blocked the road. The machine had no visible lights, but it did have some luminous decals that reflected light. Our client said he first noticed the reflectors immediately before the crash. He barely had time to put on his brakes.

The sheriff's report verified there were no barricades or warning signs at the intersection of the town road and the highway. The sheriff was our key witness in this regard. However, the Sheriff's written report also stated that the next night when he approached the accident scene to further his investigation, he could see the reflectors with his automobile's low beam from the top of the hill, *"a quarter of a mile away"*. I interviewed the sheriff and he did not back down. My client also remained firm that he could not see the reflectors until immediately before the accident. As the trial approached, I interviewed the sheriff on two other occasions. On the last occasion, he invited me to his home for dinner. I was amazed to find that neither defense counsel nor the insurance adjustor for the contractor had ever interviewed him.

Through pre-trial discovery, we found out that the defendant had hired a photographer to make a video motion picture of the reflectors at dusk. The video was taken first with the photographer's bright lights on, and then with the dim lights. Even though the insurance company had retained the photographer, it was not unethical for me to interview him before the trial. I drove out to see him and brought along a copy of the video I obtained from the defendant through discovery. After viewing the video, the photographer gave me a sworn statement verifying that his video showed that at 50 miles per hour with dim lights, the reflectors were first visible 50 to 75 feet away; with bright lights on, 100 to 125 feet away.

On the first morning of the trial, I asked the sheriff if he would come to court early. When he arrived, I told him I was going to place him on the stand and ask him only about the absence of the barricade. I told him since we felt he was mistaken about the distance from which the reflectors could be seen on approach, I would not question him about this. When he arrived, I told him I had a witness to put on the stand before he testified. Much to the surprise of defense counsel, I called the photographer which the defense had hired and had him run the video and verify that the reflectors of the road machine could be seen on low beam from only 50 to 75 feet away. The defense lawyer had planned to interview the photographer before the defendant's case in chief. As it turned out opposing counsel never had a chance to talk to him. The law required the reflectors on a stationary vehicle to be seen at a minimum of 200 feet.

As our next witness I called the sheriff, who had sat in the courtroom when the photographer testified. I questioned him, as I promised, only about the absence of the barricade at the entry of the town road onto the state highway. On cross-examination, defense counsel, with the sheriff's report in hand, asked the sheriff whether he had visited the accident scene the night following the accident. He acknowledged that he had. Then came the frightening question: How far away could you see the reflectors as you approached them that next evening? The sheriff's answer: "About 50 to 75 feet." Defense counsel, for whatever reason, did not attempt to refresh the sheriff's recollection or impeach him from the state report. The point is: If a witness you feel is mistaken can be exposed to other testimony which you feel is more accurate, perhaps you can persuade the witness of the possible mistake. Remember estimates of speed and distance are only opinions and witnesses can often be wrong.

Avoid Leading Questions Unless Necessary

Many lawyers fail to use proper leading questions on either direct or cross-examination, and lose the persuasive effect of the witness's answers. This is especially true on direct examination where the use of leading questions is generally prohibited. Even if the opposing lawyer fails to object, jurors are wise enough to know that it is the lawyer testifying and not the witness. Of course, on direct examination, when the judge sustains the objection that counsel is "leading the witness" it certainly doesn't help your case in the eyes of the jury. When I first started trying cases, a friendly judge corrected me and suggested in front of the jury, that I should always ask questions beginning with words that start "W" or "H". ("What", "when", "where", "who", "why" and "how"). I think it is wise to apply the same rule on cross-examination where possible. The jury may resent efforts to put words in the witness's mouth. However, sometimes leading questions to an adverse witness are the only safe approach.

Do Not Try To Impress The Jury With Your Erudition

When lawyers call an expert witness, such as a physician or an engineer, it is important for them to thoroughly understand the subject matter involved, but a lawyer should not make the common mistake in trying to impress the jury with their newly acquired learning. Many lawyers feel they have mastered medical terms and should use these terms to examine professional witness. Specialized terminology may go over the jury's heads. The result is that the jury knows very little about what the lawyer has tried to prove. It is important to understand the subject matter, so that a lawyer can make certain that the testimony is conveyed in common terms to the lay jury. If the physician or engineer answers in technical terms counsel should use the opportunity to have the witness spell out the "ordinary meaning" to "ordinary folks." For example, the surgeon might testify that he performed a laminectomy on your client. Counsel could say: "Doctor, I'm not sure what that means. Could you break that down in lay terminology so that I can better understand. I'm certain the jury would appreciate that, too." Two points: first, the jury needs to understand and, second, the jury is made to feel that counsel is no more learned than they are. I have seen lawyers cross-examine physicians in strictly medical terms and it goes completely over the jurors' heads.

THE RELUCTANT OR RECALCITRANT WITNESS

There are few lay witnesses who relish the idea of appearing in court. Most citizens are frightened to come to court. They have seen enough Perry Mason shows to know that "shrewd lawyers" possess the tools to make them look foolish when they take the stand. Lay witnesses also fear the formality of court proceedings, taking an oath, and often the stern judge who runs the court. The lay witness is often intimidated by the jury as well. But beyond all that, many witnesses feel their time is too valuable to get involved in somebody else's problems.

Every lawyer needs psychological tools to persuade and reassure material witnesses of the importance of appearing in court. Logic does not always work. Some witnesses are unmoved by discussions about a citizen's duty or the suggestion that if "they" were a party who depended on a witness, they would feel terribly distressed if the witness refused to testify. Even though you can subpoena a witness (and there are good reasons to not subpoena every witness), it is essential that you have a cooperative, unresentful witness on the stand.

I list the following suggestions as pointers from my experience on getting reluctant witnesses to testify.

Be Polite, But Firm

In one of my cases, the only neutral witness to a collision between a bus and a passenger car refused to appear in court. I represented the bus company. The focal issue was who entered the intersection against the red light. The neutral witness owned a bar on the street corner bordering the intersection of the collision, had been walking his dog early one morning when he observed the collision. We found his name on the police report. From the very beginning of the investigation, he had refused to give our investigator a statement. At the trial, the plaintiff testified that he entered the intersection on a green light and was hit by the bus. Our driver stated the opposite. The passengers on the bus did not know who had the green light.

The second night of the trial, I decided to try to talk to the tavern owner. I went to the bar at about 10:30 at night. I bought a beer and waited until 11:30 when the bar cleared out. I introduced myself to the owner and told him why I was there. At first he was very hostile. I bought a second beer and asked if I could visit with him about the case. He finally warmed up and admitted he had seen the accident. He was a typical, cigar-smoking character, right out of a Damon Runyon story. He stated he knew all the judges, the mayor and the city council. I pleaded to his civic spirit. Finally, he admitted that the bus driver had the green light and that the automobile had entered on a red light. I told him where the court room was and what time I needed him. He said he would think about it and *might* come to the courthouse the next day. I left at 12:30 a.m. full well knowing that my bar owner "friend" would never show up.

The next morning I called the sheriff and had a subpoena issued for the bar owner to appear at 9:00 a.m. Court started at 9:30. The bar owner appeared in a fit of anger. He told me that the deputy sheriff had gotten him out of bed and that if I placed him on the stand I would regret it. He said he would testify the driver of the auto had the green light. Suddenly, I turned on him and said, "And that my friend would be perjury. I am now going to have the sheriff escort you to the judge in his chambers and have you tell the judge what you just told me. Either that or you take the stand and tell the truth." He took the stand and told the truth.

Two other incidents make my point. I once needed to show that a contractor had cut a curb in a city sidewalk to construct a new driveway. My client had run into an unmarked ditch which was parallel to the highway. After conducting an interview, I subpoenaed the deputy clerk to show that the City had no record of a permit being issued to make a curb cut for the property. Under the municipal ordinance, failure to obtain a permit for a curb cut could constitute under relevant circumstances negligence per se. The deputy city clerk appeared in court under the issued subpoena. However, sitting with her in the courtroom was the deputy city attorney. He was the brother of one of the defense counsel for the contractor we were suing. I knew him. I walked over and said to him, "Bernie, what are you doing here?" He said, "The deputy clerk knows nothing. The records are unavailable to show whether the contractor obtained a permit or not." I turned to him and whispered to him: "Bernie, I'll give you one minute to get the hell out of this courtroom. Otherwise, you are going to be my first witness and I'm going to prove you are the brother of the defense counsel and that you have instructed the clerk to conceal the true record." I walked away. He flushed and as the judge entered the court room, Bernie left. The clerk testified truthfully that no permit had been issued.

On a slip and fall case, my client was suing a local hospital. The treating doctor had prepared a report stating that my client had a 20% permanent disability resulting from a broken leg caused by the fall. I knew that the treating doctor was chief of staff of the hospital being sued. When the case went to trial, I had arranged for the doctor to appear at 2:00 in the afternoon. During the noon recess, I received a call from him. He told me, "Don, I've been going over my notes and I have decided that I was mistaken in giving this person a 20% disability. I will have to testify that she has no disability at all." I bristled. I said, "Doctor, I am well aware that you are Chief of Staff of the hospital. Since I last talked to you, you have obviously become aware that this case is against the hospital. If you testify there is no disability, I will ask the court permission to treat you as an adverse witness, show you are chief of staff and produce your report which shows a 20% disability. And I will ask you about the telephone conversation we are now having." The doctor then said, "Would you settle for 10%?" I said, "Sure." I called him to the stand and asked if my client was permanently disabled. He said, "She is." I rested my case.

A Little Psychology Goes A Long Way

Lawyers should always remember there is a little vanity in everyone. In a case in which my client had experienced surgery for a herniated disc, his physician refused to allow an interview before trial. "I'll come to court and tell you what I know. That's all." I subpoenaed the doctor to make certain that he would appear. His negative attitude was obvious. He obviously did not like lawyers. I tried to no avail to make him aware that it was not my case that was being tried, but his patient's case.

I set the subpoena a half an hour ahead of court. I wanted to make one last attempt to talk to him about his testimony. This worked to a limited extent. I explained my concern that the jury might not fully understand what a herniated disc is and asked if he would use some medical drawings and charts to explain the injury to the jury. The doctor once again became irate and said, "I refuse to use those trick devices simply to help a lawyer try his case." I stated I was sorry he felt that way and reluctantly entered the courtroom.

As I called the doctor to the stand, I was extremely concerned whether the doctor would become so recalcitrant that he would harm my client's case. I began questioning the doctor to lay foundation for his expert opinion and then as we proceeded, I became aware of something to which I had not given much prior thought.

As I began to explore the background of the witness and mentioned his training and degrees, he became very proud and confident. I was aware he liked to tell about his credentials and professional standing. I then went beyond laying the normal foundation and began to explore the awards and special recognition he had received in his field. I asked him about his board certification and the significance of the certification in his field. I brought out that he had taught medicine in his specialty at the local medical university. It was obvious he was a man possessed of great pride. After taking over twenty minutes to get through all of this, I asked him to describe his patient's injury. I'll never forget his response: "I noticed you have some charts and graphs there; if I could use those I think I could better explain the plaintiff's injury."

Do I need say more!

Protect Your Flanks—Don't Discount The Personal Interest Of The Witness

I once represented a taxi cab driver who had been seriously injured in a collision between his cab and another vehicle. He had a passenger in the taxi who received some minor injury. My client spent several weeks in the hospital. The taxi company had a complete investigation file. All the evidence favored my client. He had entered an intersection from the right of the approaching driver. Under the law of the state, this provided him the right of way. All witnesses testified that the other vehicle entered the intersection clearly in excess of the speed limit. The passenger who had been injured, was represented by another lawyer. However, at the time I went to trial, she had not brought any suit against anyone. She had earlier given a statement to the cab company which verified the driver of the cab had entered the intersection first at a moderate rate of speed. She related she had not seen the other vehicle approaching from the left until immediately before impact. Her lawyer did not want me to talk to her before her testimony, but verified that she would testify according to her statement. I should have realized that all was not well.

CHAPTER IV — THE WITNESS

My direct examination of the witness was uneventful. On cross-examination of the witness by the other driver's lawyer, the unexpected occurred. She was asked whether she was looking to her left as the other car approached. She said: "No." When asked "What were you doing?" I knew we were in trouble. She replied: "I was talking to the driver of the cab." "What was the driver of the cab doing?" She replied: "He had his head completely turned in my direction away from the other vehicle and was talking to me!" Under the law of the state, the cab company owed a passenger the duty to exercise the highest degree of care.

Despite my client's vehemently denying the truth of the passenger's statement, we lost the case. Notwithstanding the defendant-driver's proven negligence, the jury found my client was guilty of contributory negligence barring his recovery. The cab company was a sure target for the passenger to make a claim against. She later sued both the cab company and the other driver. I made a mistake in relying upon her original statement. I should have taken her deposition before trial; at least that way I could have anticipated what obstacles we would face.

CHAPTER V
THE TRIAL JUDGE

THE ROLE OF THE TRIAL JUDGE

THE DIGNITY OF THE TRIAL JUDGE

JUDGES ARE HUMAN, TOO
"Ya Gotta Know The Territory"

JUDICIAL BIAS
The Swedish "Connection"
The Judge "Advocate"
Choosing the Judge
The "Home Town" Judge
The Hostile Judge
Handling Judicial Bias—Protect Your Client
Judicial Interference
The Eccentric Judge
"Political" Bias
The "Kept" Judge
The Lazy Judge
The Cost Of Delay
The Incompetent Judge
Instructions
Mr. Good Guy
Common Sense
The Senile Judge
The Writ of Prohibition
The Dishonest Judge

THE JUDGE AS A FACT FINDER

THE ROLE OF THE TRIAL JUDGE

The state or federal trial judge serves the most important role in dispensing justice in our judicial system. The trial judge can grant summary judgment, dismiss the case before trial on legal grounds, and grant judgments as a matter of law after the plaintiff rests or even after the verdict is reached. In sentencing in criminal cases, the trial judge has great discretion even under criminal justice systems that utilize sentencing guidelines. In rendering a sentence in a criminal case, the trial judge must balance the needs of society in terms of punishment and retribution with the needs of the convicted individual and the rippling effects of the sentence on his or her family. The trial judge's discretion in this regard falls short of being awesome, and it should not be otherwise.

Moreover, the public view of the court system is largely shaped by the trial judge. Trial judges deal with more members of the public than appellate judges or even the Justices of the Supreme Court of the United States. Jurors meet only trial judges; witnesses and most lawyers encounter the trial judge on a daily basis. Citizens appraise the justice system by their first hand observation of the trial court.

The trial judge's job is more difficult than that of the appellate judge, in that he or she must act alone, and cannot rely on others to share in the opinion writing or the decision making. The trial judge generally handles a much greater volume of cases and plays a much more direct role in the decisional process in any kind of litigation. On a legal ruling, the trial judge's decision in many areas of the law is unreviewable—the admission or exclusion of evidence generally lies within his or her discretion, and the trial judge's findings of fact cannot be reversed without a finding of clear error. Although the trial court's ruling of law is reviewed de novo, an appellate court will affirm the trial court even if there is error unless the trial court's ruling is so prejudicial that a new trial is required. Appellate courts reverse a very small percentage of cases. After all, the justice system could not exist if the reversal rate of trial courts were higher. Principles of finality govern the thinking of appellate courts; cases should not be reversed unless there is clear prejudicial error.

THE DIGNITY OF THE TRIAL JUDGE

Considering the important role of the trial judge, it seems to me that society should strive to obtain the most highly qualified persons to serve as trial judges. In my view, good trial judges should have the following qualities: that they be knowledgeable, organized, patient and compassionate to their fellow human beings, with a genuine sense of fairness and, above all else, abundant common sense. The combination of these attributes creates a balanced judicial temperament. Great trial judges strive for excellence in whatever they do. They realize the importance of their role in society, knowing that the appearance of fairness and neutrality is just as important to our justice system as justice itself. As a lawyer when I appeared before a hard working, knowledgeable, fair trial judge, I worked with greater zeal to try my case and to strive for greater excellence in presenting my case.

Because the public's perception of the justice system is shaped by the trial judge, I believe that trial courts proceedings should be conducted with the same formality as appellate courts. After I became an appellate judge, a friend of mine was telling me about the municipal court on which he sat, where citizens could appear and argue claims, without counsel, up to $1,000. He described his role in self-demeaning terms, contrasting his position as a municipal judge with that of a federal appeals judge. He told me as a small claims judge he saw no need to wear a robe or conduct the proceeding with any degree of formality. My response was that he was dead wrong. I explained that he had a greater opportunity than I did to demonstrate to ordinary citizens the importance of our justice system. I suggested that small claims judges wear a robe and maintain a certain decorum. Because many members of the public would never be involved or observe the legal process except in the small claim court, I told him it was vital that all citizens appreciate the solemn demeanor of the proceedings. Months later, he informed me he had persuaded his colleagues on the municipal court to wear robes and that he felt it enhanced the prestige of the court.

I recall a short anecdote about a well-respected federal trial judge from Nebraska, Robert Van Pelt. Judge Van Pelt was one of the most conscientious trial judges I have ever encountered. I tried many cases before him. One Sunday morning at my church during a men's prayer breakfast, each man in attendance was asked to mention the name of a person who had recently influenced his life. One of the men said

"Judge Robert Van Pelt." Afterwards, I approached this individual, who I knew was engaged in business and was not a lawyer, and said: "How do you know Judge Van Pelt?" He replied that about a month ago he had been called for jury service in the federal court. He had never met the judge, but had sat as a juror on one of his cases. He said, "I have never been so impressed with a man who was so fair and knowledgeable, so patient and understanding, so considerate of the lawyers and the witnesses, as well as the jurors." He continued saying, "It was obvious to all of us on the jury the judge possessed the greatest integrity and concern in seeing that both sides received a fair trial. After that experience, I decided I would like to try to emulate those characteristics in my business. He greatly influenced my life."

If only all trial judges could have the characteristics of Judge Van Pelt.

JUDGES ARE HUMAN, TOO

Just as there are many different kinds of lawyers, there are many different kinds of judges. Many judges are good and fair, some are not. I firmly believe that the vast majority of judges are fair and attempt to do a good job on the bench. However, trial judges come from all walks of life and from many varied backgrounds. They each are products of their own life experiences which form different attitudes, philosophies and biases.

As a lawyer when I would voir dire jurors, I told them "that all of us are products of our own experiences, but under oath as a juror, you will be asked to put aside your own experiences, biases and prejudices and to try the case solely on the evidence and the law that the judge gives you." Realistically, this is impossible. Taking the oath cannot make a person forget his own experiences. However, the admonition did serve to appeal to a juror's sense of fair play and to reveal prospective jurors' hidden prejudices. Unfortunately, lawyers do not have a similar opportunity to voir dire the trial judge. Wouldn't it be interesting if a lawyer could examine a judge with questions such as "Can you be fair *under the circumstances of this case?*"

Trial judges quickly gain a reputation with members of the bar. Lawyers often say that "judge so and so" is "a good judge," "a bad judge," "a mean judge," "a fair judge," etc. But whatever the judge's reputation, the lawyer must accept the judge as she or he is. A trial lawyer's biggest problem is how to handle the unfair or abusive judge. I use the term "abusive" in a broad sense. The term includes a judge who is biased toward one side as well as a judge who is rude and belligerent to lawyers or the parties during a trial.

"Ya Gotta Know The Territory"

I like to tell law students that they should remember this refrain from Meredith Wilson's memorable lyrics in the stage and movie production of *The Music Man*. Trial judges are not robots. Each judge has a distinct personality and acts in accord with his or her own sense of judicial discretion and within his or her own sense of what justice is all about. The following illustrates my point: two judges within the same jurisdiction where I practiced exercised different procedures as to whether counsel should stand or sit while questioning witnesses. The neophyte counsel who dared not to informally inquire before trial as to the practice always drew a sharp comment (in front of the jury) as to which practice was to be observed.

My early mentors taught me to respect the judiciary and my courtroom behavior as counsel was always governed by this early discipline. However, this does not mean a lawyer should become a whipping post for the judge who delights in abusing trial counsel. Every lawyer, "with all due respect to the court," must stand up and assert the rights of his client. Some lawyers are intimidated by judges who become openly critical of objections. On appeal, the lament of the lawyer, who tells the appellate court he did not object to a question or to the judge's wrongful interference in the trial because the trial judge was critical of those who object in his or her court, carries little weight. The lawyer who says, "I didn't object because I have to try other cases before the same judge," provides a lame excuse. Every lawyer owes his client more.

JUDICIAL BIAS

My first experience before a "trial judge" was not a good one. I had been out of law school barely two weeks and hardly knew the floor in the building where my law firm was located when a junior partner asked me if I would like to try a case before a Justice of the Peace Court in a small nearby town. He told me it was a "sure winner." As the day approached, tension and sheer excitement mounted. Our client was the Jewel Tea Company, which sold groceries from house to house. I still remember my childhood excitement when the Jewel Tea driver would call at our home on Saturday afternoon with all kinds of baked goods.

In the case I was to try, the Jewel Tea vehicle was traveling down a country road when a farmer emerged from his driveway and drove into the side of the passing Jewel Tea panel truck. I had pictures of the Jewel Tea truck which showed damage on the right front door and fender. The farmer had filed a suit for $447. (I still recall the amount). We had filed a counterclaim for the damage to the truck for approximately $200.

I remember climbing the outside stairway in the little, white framed house where the Justice of the Peace worked and lived. The small "courtroom" was adorned only with shades on the windows (no curtains). In the small room were two wooden tables where the litigants and counsel could sit. The Justice of the Peace sat behind a larger table upon which a green glass shade and lamp, with brass pull chain, rested along side several long quill writing pens and a bottle of black ink. Behind the table was an old roll top desk. With two lawyers, two witnesses, and the Justice of the Peace, the room seemed very crowded. In the courtroom, my adversary introduced himself to me for the first time. He was the town's leading lawyer (it had only three). He had been the county attorney for several years and at 45 years of age had gained a state-wide reputation for being a "nice guy" and a solid lawyer.

We sat in the courtroom for about five minutes when the door from the next room opened. The Justice of the Peace made his entrance. At age 82, he had been Justice of the Peace for over 30 years. He was not a lawyer. A Justice of the Peace in those days did not have to have a law degree. The position of Justice of the Peace has since been abolished in most states—for reasons that will become obvious by the end of this story.

The judge sat down and with a trembling, soft voice said: "Gentlemen, I am ready to hear your opening statements." My adversary rose and began to speak quietly. As he went along his voice rose with emotion. He laid out the facts accurately until he came to the collision. All of a sudden, with a loud and excitable voice, he exclaimed that the Jewel Tea driver, approaching the driveway at a 90 degree angle, had with great speed crashed into the farmer's front end. He sounded as if he were Clarence Darrow pleading the case for Nathan Leopold. He then turned to me and pointed with an accusatory finger, stating that "this large corporation and their corporate attorney" (it momentarily made me feel important) had caused this great injustice to "this poor farmer" requiring him to come to court and sue for his expenses in getting his car repaired. He demanded that justice be served and the farmer be awarded the full $447.

The time had come for my opening statement. I nervously arose and began to explain to the court that I would offer the pictures of the vehicles which vividly displayed the only way the collision could actually have happened. I carefully pointed out the farmer's version was an impossibility. As I spoke, I was standing approximately three feet from the desk of the Justice of the Peace. I noticed he opened a gray ledger book and with one of his quill pens began to write laboriously. The judge was not even listening to me. I moved closer to his desk and carefully set out the evidence the defense would produce. Looking over the green shaded lamp, I observed what the Justice of the Peace was writing. Before I sat down, I could read the entire entry. He had been writing in the "Judgment Book" and the inscription read as follows: "Judgment for the plaintiff in the amount of $447; counterclaim of defendant dismissed."

I was, of course, flabbergasted! I said: "Judge, I hope you are going to hear the evidence?" He responded: "Of course, that is why we are here." And I thought—well, perhaps I am wrong. Perhaps, I misunderstood what the writing meant.

The trial began with the plaintiff presenting his version. He testified he had stopped at the end of his driveway and the Jewel Tea truck had run into him. I then, masterfully I thought, cross-examined the farmer showing his testimony to be nonsensical. The plaintiff then rested his case.

I placed the Jewel Tea driver on the stand. I offered the photographs, which the Justice of the Peace carefully marked as exhibits. In the course of the next hour, I presented Jewel Tea's case, and both sides made final arguments. The Justice of the Peace took the case under advisement and told us he would let us know the result in a few days. Two days later I received a postcard through the mail. It was illegibly typed, but the message was clear. It repeated word for word the ledger inscription written by the Justice of the Peace during my opening statement. "Judgment for the plaintiff in the amount of $447; counterclaim of defendant dismissed."

In just two weeks time from my graduation from law school, my idealism of the law was shattered. From this initial experience, I learned several lessons which have remained with me through the years: (1) the value of advocacy; (2) the fact that a little local knowledge goes a long way; (3) that the law is not always perfect, nor is it always fair; and (4) who the trial judge is makes a big difference in the results of litigation. Once again the observation can be made that legal results and consequences more often turn on the human characteristics of the diverse people involved in the process than anything else. The more a lawyer can understand, appreciate and *anticipate* the personality of the trial judge, the more successful he or she will become.

Every lawyer will agree that suggesting to a judge that he or she might be biased in a particular case is not the most popular claim to make. Appellate courts occasionally reverse a judgment where judicial bias is considered so prejudicial that the trial was not fair. Lawyers sometimes move to disqualify a trial judge, but they do so reluctantly because when unsuccessful, they often fear the wrath of the judge during the trial. However, it is essential to remember that judges are not immune from personal biases and prejudices simply because they are judges. The difficulty facing counsel is where hidden bias cannot openly be challenged. The lawyer must confront such bias with every resource available.

The Swedish "Connection"

I was second-chair to my mentor, a skilled trial practitioner, in one of my early trials. The plaintiff was a native born Swede by the name of Yalmar Hanson. He brought suit against our client, the Street Railway Company, claiming that he was sitting at a red light on the street by the streetcar tracks, and the streetcar ran into the back end of his vehicle. He claimed he had fractured his leg. His doctor interpreted the healed fracture line as being a recent injury. The judge, who was Irish, had served on the bench too long. He was crotchety and impatient and did not like to try cases. While the plaintiff was on the stand, his lawyer, who was obviously inexperienced, made the error of searching his file for an exhibit to be marked. He had evidently misplaced the exhibit. There was a long lull in the testimony while the lawyer looked for the lost exhibit. The judge finally blurted out "Come on—let's get this two-bit case over with." The lawyer apologized; he became flustered and never did offer the exhibit. A recess followed.

At the recess, my senior associate, who was well-acquainted with the judge, wandered "ex parte," without opposing counsel, into the judge's chambers and stated: "Judge, what did you say that for? If we win, the Supreme Court could reverse the whole case on appeal for what you said."

The judge flushed and then told this story that I have long remembered: "Well, I know I shouldn't have said what I did. However, when my wife and I were first married back in 1919, we had a Swedish maid. She wasn't married and she was a good maid. One day I came home and she said that she was going to have to quit because she had become pregnant." And then he startled us both and said: "I haven't liked Swedes ever since."

The Judge "Advocate"

The worst form of judicial bias occurs when the judge enters into the adversary fray and takes sides with one side or the other. This often happens in a criminal trial where the judge feels that the prosecutor is unable to prosecute the case effectively against the skilled criminal lawyer appearing for the defendant. The jury quickly discovers which side the judge favors. This type of bias often is not reflected on the transcript sufficient for the appeal court to reverse. Oftentimes, the bias is evident from the record. In one case I sat on with the Court of Appeals, the trial judge refused to allow both counsel to question the witnesses. He stated the public issue was so great that he was going to call his own witnesses and do his own questioning. Our court issued a writ of prohibition and removed him from the case. At that time we observed:

> [The trial judge] seems to have shed the robe of the judge and to have assumed the mantle of the advocate. The court thus becomes lawyer, witness and judge in the same proceeding, and abandons the greatest virtue of a fair and conscientious judge—impartiality.

> A judge best serves the administration of justice by remaining detached from the conflict between the parties. As Justice McKenna stated long ago, "[T]ribunals of the country shall not only be impartial in the controversies submitted to them but shall give assurance that they are impartial. . . ." *Berger v. United States*, 255 U.S. 22, 35-36 (1921). When the judge joins sides, the public as well as the litigants become overawed, frightened and confused. *Reserve Mining Co. v. Lord*, 529 F.2d 181 (8th Cir. 1976).

JUDICIAL BIAS

Choosing The Judge

Counsel should carefully evaluate which forum is more likely to bring a successful outcome. Often times the defense counsel must make a decision in evaluating whether to remove a state filed claim to federal court, or whether to request a transfer of a case to a more convenient or proper venue. In making this choice, the first question is where jurisdiction (authority to hear) and venue (situs of the court) of the suit properly lie. Once those options are defined, counsel must consider various other factors: choice of law, the convenience of the forum, factors governing the selection of the jury, size of the jury, availability of lawyer voir dire, and the locale where the prospective jurors live. In my view, however, these considerations are secondary to the most important consideration of all: who will be the judicial officer to preside over the litigation.

In litigation, certain judges gain a reputation with the bar as being for the plaintiff or the defendant, or as being a "law and order" judge. Lawyers frequently refer to judges as a "plaintiff's judge" or "defendant's judge." In smaller communities this reputation is well known and often used by lawyers to their advantage. Lawyers use a variety of techniques to get their cases before a judge they feel will favor their side. Many courts have adopted procedures to prevent this, but it still happens.

When I first started practice I was assigned by a junior partner in the law firm to defend the street railway company in cases involving property damage. These cases were a great way to learn trial procedures; the rules of evidence applied, and I had to prepare witnesses for testimony as well as conduct direct and cross-examination. These cases were all tried in municipal court before a single judge. I had tried twelve cases in a row and was pleased that I had been successful in all twelve in getting a defendant's verdict. One day, I tried a case that I thought I should win but I lost. I was discussing the case before the junior partner who had assigned these cases to me. He told me "You have tried all your cases before Judge X; I always told you to try to get the case assigned to Judge X, but this time you had Judge Y." I acknowledged the same but asked, "What's the difference? They both seemed like good judges to me." He replied "Judge X's brother works for the street railway company." It seemed that we always won the close cases before Judge X. All of my satisfaction for winning the twelve cases went out the window. I was ashamed that I had been taken advantage of along with the opposing counsel and his client.

Years ago, in a malpractice case in state court in which I represented the plaintiff, two defense lawyers filed motions challenging my client's petition. In state practice at that time, the motions were called "motions to make more definite and certain." These motions, which were often eight to ten pages long, were verbose and redundant. Under the state court rule, the trial date couldn't be set until the plaintiff could get a judge to hear argument on any interlocutory motion the defendant might have filed. This procedure allowed defense lawyers to engage in a delaying tactic. It seldom accomplished any meaningful result. The general routine was to calendar the motions for oral argument by calling the calendar clerk and once being assigned a judge, serving notice on opposing counsel to appear.

In the malpractice case, I served the notice and the designated time arrived and I appeared in the judge's courtroom. My opposing counsel were not present, but one of them had left a phone number with the message they would be in the calendar clerk's office to obtain the assignment. It dawned on me that the judge assigned was reputed to be a "plaintiff's judge" and even on a meaningless motion the two defense attorneys were going to try to place their motions before a more favorable judge to hear the motions. I went to the calendar clerk's office. The defense lawyers explained they wanted a different judge to hear the arguments. They said they wanted Judge "B." Judge B was a fair judge but did have a reputation as a defendant's judge. I told them that I had been assigned Judge A and that I had not purposely chosen Judge A. I was also concerned that Judge B had not scheduled the arguments and that the case would be further delayed. They assured me that they had checked and Judge B was available.

The calendar clerk, who was 82 years old and very forgetful, intervened and stated he thought we should draw the judge's name out of a hat. We agreed. Then the clerk wrote the full names of Judge A and Judge B on slips of paper. He also took a blank slip and placed all three slips of paper in his hat. At this point, the three of us were somewhat quizzical as to how the drawing would be conducted. The clerk then asked each of us to draw a slip of paper from the hat. I drew Judge B's name. My adversaries drew the other slips, one drawing Judge A's name and the other drawing the blank paper. The clerk took a yellow pad and asked each of us the name we had drawn. He laboriously recorded the score, Judge A recorded one mark, Judge B one mark, and the blank one mark. The clerk then astounded us all by announcing: "It's a tie, we will have to do it again." By the time each of us had recovered from hysterical laughter, the clerk repeated the same process and announced once again: "It's another tie."

I finally agreed to go to Judge B's court. The defense attorneys argued their motions for over an hour. Judge B overruled their motions in their entirety.

The "Home Town" Judge

One reason trial lawyers often retain local counsel when a case must be tried away from their home locale is to give the jury the impression that a local lawyer is involved in the case and that the out of town lawyer is not trying to "pick on" a local citizen. In smaller communities, the local lawyer often knows some of the prospective jurors and can provide a greater insight as to the objective fairness of the juror. In some cases, a local lawyer is an asset in obtaining a fair trial from local judges. For whatever reason, some trial judges treat nonresident lawyers with hostility. This may happen in subtle ways. I have appeared before judges who always called the nonresident lawyer as "Mister" Jones or Smith (always using the last name) while he would address the local attorney as Tom or Bill (always using the first name). The jurors could easily perceive the difference in the judge's attitude toward each lawyer.

I recall one case I tried out in a small country town in Nebraska. The opposing lawyer lived in the next county and tried many cases before the local district judge. In the courtroom, he was very theatrical and dramatic, always putting on a great show. However, because he did not know any of the local jurors, I did not think I needed a local lawyer to assist me in the case. During the trial, the judge showed his partiality and friendship to my opponent. The judge used his first name, while being very curt with me. He continually accused me in front of the jury of taking too much time in proving my case. We came to the time for the closing argument. As the plaintiff's counsel, I made my final argument first. My opponent was theatrical throughout his argument, concluding with an emotional plea for justice. As he concluded his argument with frenzied emotion, he began to gasp for air and fell back in his chair and reached out with a trembling hand to sip from his glass of water at the counsel table. I had seen the same sideshow before and knew it was all an act. However, the jury did not and I am certain there were some jurors that were concerned whether he was going to live or die. All of their eyes, except mine, were staring intently at him. At that precise time the judge looked down at him, while he was still breathing heavily, and said "John boy, that was the best jury argument I have ever heard." When the jury went back to the jury room, I moved for a mistrial. It was overruled. I went back to my hotel room to pack. In forty minutes, the bailiff called and told me that the jury had rendered a verdict for good old "John boy."

The Hostile Judge

One reason for filing a case in federal court, particularly when you are representing a nonresident citizen, is to avoid possible local prejudice a local jury might have against a nonresident. Federal juries are chosen from a much broader geographic area than state juries. Unfortunately, I have found some federal trial judges, like some state court judges, do not like to have nonresident lawyers coming into their court. Some federal trial judges resent lawyers from a different state "clogging their docket." They make this known by stating at pretrial that they don't think much of the case or commenting "why isn't this case in state court." I often had the feeling that some of the federal trial judges in different states were giving me an early message that they were in charge and the trial would proceed according to their rules. It always seemed to me that the brunt of these messages were directed at the out-of-state lawyer.

There is no doubt that some trial judges often display a mean and hostile attitude at one or both lawyers in certain trials. I intend no general disparagement, but any lawyer who has spent a lifetime in litigation will verify there are certain judges who manifest little civility to or respect for the trial bar who assume an arduous responsibility in proving or in defending a client's interests.

So there is no misunderstanding, I do not criticize a trial judge who runs a "tight ship" by eliminating side exchanges by counsel with one another or who prevents lawyers from arguing objections in front of the jury. I also do not criticize the trial judge who reprimands counsel for obvious judicial misconduct. My concern is with the harassment of counsel, often times both counsel, in front of the jury, where the trial judge is constantly reprimanding lawyers for everything, beginning with voir dire, the questions asked of witnesses, and extending through the closing argument.

I often sense that judges who give lawyers a hard time are the ones who have had little trial experience themselves. It is indeed embarrassing to a lawyer, in front of the jury or his client, to constantly be criticized by the trial judge. I doubt if trial judges who display such hostility have ever experienced that humiliation. If they had, they would never do so in their own courtrooms.

I recall trying a case in federal court in out-state New York. Whatever I did in the trial beginning with the opening statement, through marking exhibits and examining witnesses was always wrong. The trial judge repeatedly corrected me, stating in front of the jury, "You may do things that way in your state but we don't do things that way here." The jury had the impression that I was trying to do something wrong.

I tried several cases in federal court in states neighboring Nebraska. One judge I appeared before was always hostile to lawyers from a different state. In one case, I represented the plaintiff, a pit mechanic who had lost his leg when a race car went out of control and struck him in the leg. We sued the race track for providing inadequate barriers around the track. Before trial, the judge opined that my client should accept a small settlement offered by the defendant. When my client and I refused, the judge made sarcastic comments to me throughout the trial such as "You may get away with that at home, but we do not do that here." The judge would interrupt my witnesses with his own objections. Often on his own, without objection from opposing counsel, he would strike a witness's answer as not responsive. After three days of trial and continued harassment, I decided to move to the second chair and let my young associate take over the trial. Things went a little better.

When we rested our case, the defense counsel moved for a directed verdict. I told my associate to argue our side of the case to the judge. The court stated he wanted *me* to argue the motion. I refused, politely, of course, saying that my associate was prepared to argue and I was not. The judge obviously wanted to argue with me and I was not about to have further confrontation. After the argument, the judge stated that it was a close question on liability and that he wanted to take a recess to think it over. When he returned, he did the unexpected. He took out a twelve page memorandum, which he obviously prepared the night before. The memo stated that the judge was dismissing the case because the amount of any verdict would not exceed ten thousand dollars and, therefore, federal jurisdiction did not exist. Our medical damages were in excess of forty-five hundred dollars and the plaintiff had lost his leg. The trial court's decision was almost ludicrous. We filed an immediate appeal. Two days later the defense counsel called me and agreed to pay us the sum that we had originally asked to settle before the trial began. It was obvious the judge was angry because we did not settle the case before trial. A short time later, I was appointed to the Circuit Court of Appeals. At my first judicial reception, this same trial judge approached my wife and told her: "Don was the finest trial lawyer who ever appeared before me." How quickly things change!

Handling Judicial Bias—Protect Your Client

I have tried several cases before judges who were obviously biased against my case. One trial judge once told me that "all personal injury claimants were like people on welfare because they all wanted something for nothing." The judge frequently directed verdicts against plaintiffs in personal injury cases. For example, this judge directed a verdict for a defendant, at the close of the plaintiff's case, where the plaintiff was crossing an intersection in the crosswalk with a green light when the approaching car ran the red light. The judge reasoned that the plaintiff failed to look and see the moving automobile. The case was reversed on appeal. I tried cases before two federal judges presiding in the same judicial district who had opposing philosophies on punishing defendants in tax evasion cases. One judge proclaimed that all tax evaders convicted in his court would be sentenced to the maximum provided by the statute. The other judge disliked the Internal Revenue Service and always placed a convicted tax evader on probation. (He had once been audited.) Many trial judge are pro-prosecution in criminal cases. On appeal, the criminal defendants often argue that these judges' trial comments were prejudicial error. In a criminal case I once reviewed on appeal, the trial judge in the presence of the jury overruled defense counsel's objection that the government had failed to establish foundation for some exhibits. The judge admonished defense counsel for making the objection, saying "everyone knows the government never lies."

If the trial judge is hostile to your case, for whatever reason, and the hostility is apparent, every lawyer owes a duty to his client to stand firm and move for a mistrial. This can be done politely and with respect. Regardless of the possible open hostility the judge might demonstrate against you or your client's case, a lawyer should always remember it is the court that deserves the respect, not necessarily the person sitting on it. The judge's demeaning of the bench is his or her personal problem. As an officer of the court, the lawyer should always be respectful. However, being respectful does not mean that the lawyer should not at all times represent fully the client's rights. If the trial judge reacts poorly, the lawyer should not be intimidated and fail to make the record for possible appeal.

Judicial Interference

I recall one case where the judge did not like my expert witness. The judge constantly interrupted the witness and inferred to the jury that he did not believe the witness. I approached the bench and asked if I might make a record outside the presence of the jury. The judge granted me leave to do so while the jury remained. I then whispered into the record (to the court reporter) that I felt the judge had prejudiced my case by his interruptions and comments. I respectfully moved for a mistrial. The judge asked the reporter to approach the bench and to quietly read the statement to him. She did so. He then told the reporter to read aloud my motion to the jury. I whispered to my associate and said to get ready to take over the case because I thought I was about to be excoriated in front of the jury. After my motion was read, the judge turned to the jury and stated: "Ladies and gentlemen of the jury, I want to apologize to you if I have said anything to give you the wrong impression by my comments. I intended in no way to take sides in this case. I was merely trying to clarify the situation so everyone would understand the testimony. The motion will be overruled and we will proceed." The trial court refrained from making further comments in the case. I learned from that experience that trial judges do respect the appellate process and will, if cautioned, respectfully try to avoid a mistrial or reversal and a later new trial.

The Eccentric Judge

The Supreme Court of the United States once observed that the right to a jury trial in a criminal case was essential to avoid abuse of power and the eccentric judge. Everyone has different definitions of what constitutes an eccentric judge. I use the term in the sense of the individual judge deviating from the common pattern or norm. I do not use the term in a critical sense. Every judge is different and some deviations in a judge's practice or behavior are to be commended. For example, I knew an excellent trial judge in Milwaukee before whom I tried cases who would never see a lawyer in his chambers without both sides present. The judge adopted this practice so that no one could ever assert that another lawyer could "back door" the judge or even have the opportunity to do so. He carried the practice to such an extreme that one time after I had moved from Milwaukee and had no pending case before him, I went to visit him at the courthouse simply to pay my regards. The bailiff told him I was there and stated my purpose and he insisted in coming out in the courtroom and sitting with me at the counsel table to simply have a visit. Rather than being offended, I have long remembered the incident and have respected him for what he conceived to be proper judicial decorum. Along the same lines, another judge told me about what a colleague, another federal judge, did the week after he was appointed to the bench. A neighbor lady had given him and his wife a box of freshly picked strawberries for dinner one evening. The judge returned the berries, explaining that as a federal judge he and his wife could no longer take gifts from friends because of the appearance of impropriety. I always thought this was an extreme reaction. However, I do not criticize the judges in either of these instances, but their respective practices were different from the norm. Judges may accept small gifts at Christmas time, but I believe that larger gifts from attorneys, such as golf shirts or even golf shoes, should be declined. Such gifts are improper and although well intended, border on the unethical.

Many trial judges, albeit in good faith, attempt to streamline the practice in their court so as to expedite their docket. Although this goal is certainly to be commended, the local rules can sometimes go too far. I earlier mentioned the judge who arbitrarily set a time limit in which the case had to be settled; failure to do so resulted in sanctions for the lawyer or the client. One trial judge had a rule that a defendant could not change his plea from not guilty to guilty unless he did so ten days in advance of trial. The panel of circuit judges on which I was sitting declared the rule invalid. Another judge required a party to receive his permission in order to file a motion for summary judgment. The district judge heard oral evidence of what the motion would address and if he felt the motion was frivolous or would be overruled, he would not give his permission to file it. After an appellate panel on which I sat issued an order to show cause as to why this rule did not contravene the Federal Rules of Civil Procedure, the district court rescinded his rule.

"Political" Bias

One of the problems lawyers face when judges run on political ballots is the direct or indirect solicitation of monies to run reelection campaigns. This is the primary problem for judges who must run for election even on nonpartisan tickets. Lawyers are frustrated in the possibility of losing a good judge because of the judge's inability or refusal to raise funds to run for reelection. I recall an instance years ago where it was "understood" that most of the firms gave to every incumbent judge who was up for reelection. However, one year there were two judges our firm felt were not worthy of retaining office, and we decided not to contribute to their campaigns. Unfortunately, the next week one of the two judges was assigned a case of mine for trial. On the day before trial, I met him on the street and he said: "Don, I noticed that you are going to try the next case on Monday. I also noticed that your opponent has given to my campaign fund but you have not. Is there any reason?" I responded: "Judge, I'm certain that is an oversight because our firm always contributes to each of the incumbent judges. I'll check into it." We sent a check over the next day. Fortunately, he was defeated. My reaction is that any system that allows this kind of fund raising should be abolished.

One time I was sitting on a three judge court, which by statute consisted of a circuit judge and two federal district judges. At the time, such a panel was appointed to hear all appeals from the orders of the Interstate Commerce Commission. This requirement has since been repealed. There was a direct appeal to the Supreme Court of the United States. Both counsel, one representing the Commission and the other representing a group of Railroads, came from Washington, D.C. The railroads had local counsel who had appeared on the pleadings throughout the preliminary filings. When the time came for oral argument, I was surprised to see the local counsel stand to introduce new local counsel. I had been appointed by a Democratic President. My two judicial colleagues had both been appointed by Republican Presidents. The new local lawyer had been a National Republican Committeeman. He introduced the out-of-state lawyer who argued the case.

After the case was over (the railroads lost), I asked local counsel why the railroads had brought in the new local lawyer. He told me that they thought they would have a better chance with the two Republican judges if the former National Republican Committeeman introduced the out-of-state railroad lawyer. I told him that I thought that was why he had appeared; I also told him that I thought that it was demeaning to the court. The three judges all were aware of the ploy, and we all resented it.

The "Kept" Judge

A judge in another state once told me that a major railroad company in his state tried to retain every good lawyer in every small town across the state in order to create conflicts of interest and thereby prevent the local bar from taking cases against the railroad. At the time, the railways frequently gave free passes to many state judges who presided over litigation involving the railways. The following true story illustrates the problem with judges accepting such gifts. Years ago a lawyer (who the railroads had not retained) represented a plaintiff in a personal injury case against the railroad. He lost at trial court. On appeal, he was called to make his argument. He approached the bench and stated: "My client does not wish in any way to offend the court, but he would like to present to each justice a five dollar gold piece as a symbol of his esteem and respect." He then placed before each of the justices a five dollar gold piece. He stated that he fully realized that he could not equal the value of the lifetime pass that each of the justices had received from the defendant railroad company, but he wanted the court to know that his client considered the court with equal respect as the railroad. The Chief Justice fumed. He announced that the court would be in recess. The story goes that once in the conference room the Chief Justice announced that the lawyer should be held in contempt. One of the cooler minds prevailed; another justice said that he thought they should adjourn the case and publicly announce that they were giving back their passes to the railroad. With the latter day revival and emphasis on judicial ethics, I would be very surprised that judges continue to accept such gifts.

The Lazy Judge

Although few, some judges are lazy. There are certain trial judges, for whatever reason, who do not like to try cases or at least difficult or long cases. Some judges lack confidence to try difficult cases. Generally, a lazy judge gains a reputation among his colleagues that he isn't interested in taking his fair share of the cases. Sooner or later the bar learns this. Lawyers generally encounter the problem where the assigned judge procrastinates setting the case for trial, always with some excuse. Recent court reforms now require trial judges to report their delinquent cases to either a court administrator or to the presiding judicial officer who will "police" the docket so as to expedite the progress of the cases.

The problem with the lazy judge is that the delays can affect or interfere with an expeditious handling of a client's case. For example, it is frustrating to the lawyer and his client when the judge has a motion or a ruling under advisement for an unreasonable length of time. There is an added problem when the motion under advisement is interlocutory and the judge's rulings are delaying any further work on the case. If the judge has under advisement a ruling on a motion to dismiss the complaint for failure to state a claim or because of some alleged statute of limitation defense, lawyers are reluctant to proceed with discovery for fear that it will be of no avail if the court dismisses the case on a pretrial basis. Over the years I have had numerous calls from lawyers relating to such concerns. In the federal courts we encourage judges to rule on such motions within sixty days, if not sooner.

The Cost Of Delay

When I was still in practice, a trial judge had not ruled on my opponent's motion to dismiss for over six months. The case was at a virtual stand still. I finally called the judge's secretary and asked whether it was possible to place the case on the next jury docket on the first of the month. The judge obliged me. He had obviously forgotten that there was a pending motion before him. When the court call came the first of the month, opposing counsel stood up and stated that the case was not ready to go to trial and that the court had pending before him the motion to dismiss which had been argued sometime ago. Much to the chagrin of opposing counsel, the court chided him and stated: "That's a poor excuse, counsel. I'll accommodate you; the motion is overruled. The case will go to the head of the trial docket." I always said that incident demonstrably illustrates the frustrations of being a trial lawyer.

Years ago I practiced before a judge who did not like to try cases. Lawyers could make any kind of excuse to get a continuance. If a lawyer stated that he had another case pending, even if before the police court or even if the assigned case had been set weeks in advance, the judge would continue the case. Whenever a case assigned to him was settled, he always asked the lawyers to come over to court and pick a jury notwithstanding the settlement. He explained that the jurors would not feel they were wasting their time if they in fact were called to start a case. His practice was then to announce to the jury that the lawyers had just settled the case. He would then go into oratory stating that without the appearance of the jurors, the case never would have settled.

Sometimes, after the jury was chosen he would not tell them of the settlement and would ask them to report the following morning for the start of trial. He always did this if there was another case ready to go to trial. The judge invariably would then tell the counsel in the next case that it was too late in the week to start another case. As I look back upon that experience, it is bewildering to me that the bar allowed him to do it. Yet everyone, including myself, was afraid to challenge his procedure. We also knew that he got credit for a case tried if in fact a jury had been selected in the case. The bottom line is that he did not want to try any case if he could possibly avoid doing so. Ironically, this judge would openly tell everyone he was seldom reversed by the Supreme Court.

One time I represented an elderly woman who had been seriously injured in an automobile accident. I discovered that the defendant had a fifty thousand dollar insurance policy. The case was worth every penny of the policy. Defense counsel had a reputation of not settling any case until trial had started. Unfortunately, the case was assigned to the docket of the judge who I just described. Every time I tried to get the case to trial, my opposing counsel would make an excuse that he was engaged in a previously scheduled trial. Finally, the jury term was about to end. If the case was not tired by the first week in June, summer recess would begin and would last until the middle of September. If my client died during the recess, the value of the case would be greatly diminished. I approached the trial judge and told him my problem. I also told him once the case was sent to trial, I was certain it would settle. He called opposing counsel, and we all agreed to set the trial for the first week in June.

I called opposing counsel on the weekend before trial. He was unwilling to settle. On Monday morning, I arrived at the courthouse and sat at the counsel table ready to start trial. The trial judge summoned me to his chambers. He stated that opposing counsel had just called him to tell him that he was still in trial in another courtroom in a case that had started a week earlier. I immediately went down to the other court. Opposing counsel was sitting second chair behind one of his young associates in a seven hundred dollar property damage case. I went back to the trial judge and told him the situation. He said there was nothing he could do and that the case would have to wait until after the summer recess. I had only one solution. I told the judge: "In all due respect, if opposing counsel is not called down to this court to start this case immediately, I am going to file a complaint against you before the State Judicial Ethics Committee." I stated that I thought it was a breach of his judicial duty to allow counsel to run his courtroom. I apologized for taking the position that I did, but that I had a duty to a deserving client. I was not going to stand by and allow opposing counsel manipulate the judicial process in the way that he was doing. The court was flabbergasted, but it worked. He ordered opposing counsel to pick a jury that afternoon. As I anticipated, opposing counsel called me over the noon hour and offered me the fifty thousand dollar policy limits.

The judge remained my friend. Several years later, I saw him shortly after I was appointed to the federal bench. He repeated to me what he had often said in the intervening years. "Don, no lawyer ever spoke to me as you did." I doubt if he ever forgave me. However, I always felt I did what was right for my client. A lawyer has a duty to zealously protect his or her client's interests and must respectfully guard the client's rights, even with a judge who the lawyer may offend.

The Incompetent Judge

Under an elective system of choosing judges, as well as under an appointive system, a few judges assume office who, for sheer lack of experience or ability, should not be judges. Often times this occurs when individuals seek the office of judge desiring the honor rather than the duties involved. Once such a judge gets into office, it is difficult to remove him or her. The lawyers' challenge is effectively dealing with the incompetent judge.

One of the most frustrating experiences a trial lawyer faces is the inexperienced judge who does not understand the rules of evidence. I have been before some trial judges who require a sidebar argument at the bench on every objection. These countless sidebars disrupt the flow of the trial and irritate the jury. The jury may take its frustration out on the lawyer who makes the objection.

I recall a trial that had a number of evidentiary questions. The trial judge did not understand the rules of evidence. Each time such an issue arose, the judge would adjourn court and take a recess. The jury was sent back to the jury room while counsel argued the admissibility of the evidence to the judge either in the courtroom or in his chambers. In another case I tried in St. Louis in federal court, the judge was old and partially senile. He constantly slept through the testimony. When an objection was made or an issue arose which needed the judge's ruling, the bailiff would go up to the bench, nudge the judge and give him a glass of water. The court reporter would stop while the judge recovered his composure. Once awakened, the judge routinely would say: "I didn't hear all of the objection. Would counsel please repeat it?" The trial lasted three weeks. The jury soon became aware of the judge's problem as well as the difficulty both counsel were having in presenting our testimony. Opposing counsel and I finally resolved, to the delight of the jury, to rule on each other objections. If I asked a question that was leading or one that was borderline seeking hearsay, counsel would object and I would say "sustained or overruled." The judge slept through it all. We were fair to each other and the jury fully appreciated our dilemma.

In an early trial before an inexperienced municipal judge where there was no jury, the plaintiff was seeking $800 from two defendants for property damage to his automobile. I represented one of the defendants and another lawyer represented the other. We made opening statements before the judge. Because the plaintiff was an innocent victim, the strategy of the two defendants was to blame each other's negligence as the cause of the collision. I made my opening statement and pointed out the other defendant as being the negligent party. Counsel for the other defendant rose and in his opening remarks said the evidence would show his client was not at fault and that the sole cause of the accident was the negligence of my client. After opening remarks, the ordinary procedure was for the plaintiff to call his first witness, but the trial judge interrupted and said: "Gentlemen, after hearing opening statements, I have determined that no evidence is needed since each of the defendants has admitted the negligence of the other defendant. I am therefore going to enter judgment against both defendants for $800." As plaintiff's counsel sat gleefully by, we tried in vain to tell the court he was wrong, but we did not succeed. Judgment was entered, without the court hearing the evidence of the opposing contentions.

I suggest that lawyers who face problems with inexperienced or incompetent judges try to anticipate evidentiary problems and write short written memorandums or briefs addressing those issues, then give them to counsel as well as to the court. This can be done before or during trial or counsel may request an oral conference at recess. The judge is given the opportunity to review the memo and to see the law supporting the lawyer's position before a problem arises. I appreciate that this cannot cover every situation.

Instructions

Another frustration for lawyers is the judge that lacks either the experience or the competency to prepare a good set of jury instructions. If you win the case, you have an even greater need for good instructions because you must defend the court's instructions on appeal. Many lawyers do not prepare requested instructions feeling that it is the judge's duty to instruct and the lawyer must only be certain that there are no errors in the instructions. Leaving the instructions solely to the judge is a grave mistake. I was early taught to prepare a full set of instructions relating to my case and to tender them to the court. My experience was that opposing counsel would seldom do the same. When I now sit as a trial judge, I find that the majority of counsel do not prepare requested instructions.

I was also taught to make my requested instructions balanced. Some lawyers' instructions are so one-sided that they are prejudicial in form and may be refused solely on that basis. A balanced instruction at least gets your theory of the case stated to the jury. Your requests can offset the deficiency of the judge who has difficulty preparing instructions. I tried a case before a federal judge in another state who had each lawyer prepare a complete set of instructions, including the introductory comments. At the instruction conference, he would use one of the counsel's instructions only by agreement of both lawyers. He used the excuse that in this way he could not be reversed on appeal because of an erroneous charge.

Another judge before whom I appeared frequently gave requested instructions verbatim. Knowing this fact, it was important to prepare balanced instructions. I was taught to tender second alternative requests. My mentor thought that if the judge did not accept the language of one of the instructions, perhaps another charge written in a different way but essentially saying the same thing might be acceptable. In one case involving the duty of a landlord to maintain in good repair a common entry way, I framed six alternative charges outlining the duty of the landlord. The judge read the first charge which I was pleased to have accepted, but then he started to read the second alternative charge. I turned to my associate and whispered: "You do not suppose he is going to read all six?" My fears were quickly confirmed. He read all six. After the jury was recessed, the opposing counsel made a vigorous objection about the prejudice resulting from reading six instructions on the landlord's duty. We agreed to compromise the favorable verdict in part because of the threat of reversal over the judge's repetitive instructions.

In another case, opposing counsel and I prepared diametrically opposite instructions regarding the governing law. The judge said to us, "you both know more about the law on this subject than I do, so I am going to give both instructions." The jury, of course, was totally confused and sent back a question to the judge as to which instruction to follow. The judge did not know either and simply refused to instruct the jury further on the issue. Fortunately, after the verdict was returned, the case was settled.

Mr. Good Guy

I have known some judges who try to be the "Good Guy" and throughout the trial will tell the jury jokes or stories. These tactics I believe bring disrespect to the court but equally relevant, such antics can easily serve to distract the jury from their responsibility and from carefully considering the evidence of the case before them. One time we were trying a case when the World Series was being played. The judge was a great baseball fan. He hated to miss the televised game. At the commencement of trial, while my adversary was ready to start his testimony for the plaintiff, the judge announced that he was certain that all the jurors wanted to be informed about the progress of the game as well. He told them that he had opened his chamber door to the side of the bench and that his bailiff was going to turn the television set on without sound. In that way he was able to watch the game and he would announce at various intervals whether there were any hits or scores as the game went along. He would actually interrupt the witnesses testimony to make his running commentary. I was dumbfounded. My astonishment was not only at the judge but at my opposing counsel who failed to make an objection or even a suggestion to the judge that this procedure interfered with the presentation of his case in chief. I was not surprised at the verdict when it was returned for my client.

Common Sense

Judges who do not have trial experience often times make rulings which lack common sense. In one case, on the eve of trial, the plaintiff called his client's doctor to arrange a time for the doctor to come to court to provide his medical testimony. Counsel found out that the doctor had had a recent heart attack and that he was confined to his home. However, the doctor's physician had given him permission to give his testimony by deposition in his own home. Plaintiff's counsel asked the trial judge's permission to take a recess after opening statements so that he could take the doctor's deposition to enter as evidence in the trial. The judge, who had primarily a real estate background, refused to give permission because it would violate his pretrial order that all discovery depositions had to be completed three months before trial. Counsel called my office. I was then Chief Judge of the Court of Appeals. Counsel asked if I would hear an emergency motion for a writ of mandamus. Plaintiff's counsel explained that he would not be able to prove his medical evidence unless he was able to take the doctor's deposition and offer his testimony at trial. I told him I would have to convene a three judge panel, but that we could do it over the lunch hour by telephone. However, I first suggested that I call the trial judge and see if it would be necessary to do so. I did just that. I explained to the judge it was difficult to convene a panel on an emergency basis and under the circumstances, I wondered if he might reconsider his ruling. I suggested that discovery deadlines for depositions may not govern an emergency case such as this. He said as long as I felt that way, he would be glad to accommodate counsel and allow the deposition.

I relate this last incident to point out to lawyers that if arbitrary and nonsensical rulings are made, the appellate court is available on an emergency basis to counteract obvious and prejudicial error. Although writs of prohibition or mandamus are seldom issued, there are times when it is necessary to seek them if the trial court's rulings are prejudicial to the client's case.

The Senile Judge

I had a client who ran a large construction company. He brought a case against the Bureau of Reclamation (the United States) growing out of a large dam construction site. I referred him to out of state lawyers, who tried the case before a federal district judge who was ninety years old and senile. He could not remember the case from one day to the next. He did not like my client. My client's name was Korshoj, but the trial judge called my client Kruchev throughout the trial. My client was a very proud person and deeply resented being called by the wrong name. After the trial on liability, the judge took a six week continuance before hearing the damage phase of the trial.

When the trial resumed, my client appeared and for the first several minutes after the lawyers had made opening remarks, the judge proclaimed that he was not familiar with the case and that he was certain that the case had been assigned to the wrong judge. The bailiff went onto the bench and whispered in the judge's ear. The judge then turned toward my client and said: "Oh yes, I now remember. This is Kruchev's case." My client was totally humiliated. Later, the judge dismissed the entire case. I read the entire record and recommended that the client not appeal. The judge had made findings of fact which were permissible under the record and which I did not believe could be reversed on appeal. Of course, the judge should never have been allowed to sit. However we could not prove this on the basis of the record. My client's faith in the court system was virtually destroyed.

This story illustrates that there are a few judges who are suffering from senility that should not be trying cases. In a given case, there is very little that can be done about it, whether in federal or state court. One way to ensure the competence of the judge is through a certification process.

In the federal system, the Chief Judge of the Circuit must certify each year whether a judge is competent to sit for the ensuing year. In the past, some Chief Judges have interpreted this rule as being a once a year certification. Once the certification is given it cannot be rescinded until the following year. I did not interpret the rule that way and at least on one occasion, I withdrew the certification during the year. A group of district judges as well as some lawyers met with me about an elderly judge who had recently had a stroke and could no longer speak. The Chief Judge of the district had asked the judge to step down, but the judge had adamantly refused. The judge was signalling the law clerk how to rule on the objections at trial and was having the deputy clerk read the instructions to the jury. The Chief Judge informed me that the judge was just getting ready to try a criminal trial where the defense of insanity had been raised and there was a great deal of community interest in the trial.

I worked on several drafts of a letter to the judge, knowing that he was a proud man and had served for a great number of years with dignity and dedication. In the letter, I told him that the nation was proud of his service but that in the interest of his health I felt it was in his best interests to withdraw his certification until he was able to regain his speech. The letter primarily praised his past judicial service. I sent the letter to him as a personal one and made no public announcement of it. A few days later, I received a call from the local radio station where the judge lived and worked. They wanted to interview me about the letter. I was surprised that they knew about the letter and asked how they received a copy of it. They informed me that the judge had called a press conference and had given them the letter. I was worried that the judge was trying to challenge my authority to withdraw his certification. Since a federal judge is appointed under the Constitution for life, I was skeptical whether Congress could delegate to a Chief Judge the authority to "remove" a federal judge from office without an impeachment proceedings. My anxiety was short lived. I asked what the judge had told them in response to the letter. They said that he was very grateful for the letter and that he thanked me for my kind words about his judicial service. He stated that the only reason he had continued on as a judge was because the court was shorthanded and he felt they needed his services. My response was "now, that is a touch of class. The judge is truly a great man."

The Writ of Prohibition

When a trial judges oversteps his authority or his jurisdiction, although it may happen infrequently, the lawyer's last resort may be to file a writ of prohibition. I only resorted to the issuance of a writ once in my thirty years on the bench. Similarly, as a lawyer, I only sought and temporarily obtained a writ of prohibition on one occasion. The incident is worth telling because it carries with it a story of how quickly and effectively the law may act in an emergency.

I had only been out of law school a little over three years. I was practicing law in Milwaukee. My senior partner, Ken Grubb, who later became a federal district judge, assigned an interesting case to me to prepare and try. Our client was the Schlitz Brewing Company, a well known producer of beer. One hot summer it had taken its used hops to a dump owned by a nearby suburban city, Wauwatosa. The ultra rays of the sun had decomposed the hops so as to emit a foul, sulphur-like smell in the neighborhood such that the residents complained. Someone at the dump got the bright idea to burn up the hops by pouring on them two tons of hydrogen sulfuric acid. Schlitz hired A.O. Smith, a large manufacturer, to dump the acid. Unfortunately, with the aid of the intense rays of the sun, a large cloud of hydrogen sulphide rose from the dump. In about an eight square block area the fallout blackened beautiful white and yellow frame houses; the residents, including many women and children, were exposed to the fumes, which caused severe intestinal symptoms.

CHAPTER V — THE TRIAL JUDGE

A class action law suit, brought by one hundred and ninety eight residents in the area was commenced against our client, Schlitz Brewery, A.O. Smith, and the City of Wauwatosa. Each of the defendants were immediately served with a motion for preliminary injunction to shut down the dump and cease dumping the hops and the acid. A scheduled hearing was immediately set before a judge. Unfortunately the judge assigned was an elderly judge, who was approaching ninety, known to be very forgetful and very political. On the day of the hearing we found the courtroom filled with the affected plaintiff citizens. Most of them were women and small children. Plaintiff's counsel began to describe to the judge all of the events and the ensuing cloud which had caused all of the houses to become black. Most of all, plaintiffs' counsel described vividly how all of the women and children had become sick on the streets and in their front yards. Counsel was very emotional and the judge was listening intently. As counsel described how the hops had been dumped by Schlitz, the elderly judge interrupted and said: "Wait a minute, you mean there is beer and beer bottles involved here and there are young children being exposed to all of this." Of course the plaintiff counsel rejoined in affirmative response.

The judge then turned to counsel and said: "Are you ready to go to trial on the merits tomorrow morning?" Once again plaintiffs' counsel said, although hesitatingly, "Oh, yes, Your Honor." The judge then announced he would start trial at 9:00 a.m. the next morning. He observed largely for the benefit of the packed courtroom, that women and children were involved and he had to act quickly to protect the welfare of these good people. We were all shocked and amazed; I arose and asked if I may be heard. I told the judge that I was speaking for all of the defendants and that the case could not possibly start the next day. None of the defendants had even had time to file responsive pleading, the issues had not been joined, and discovery had yet to be taken. I then stated that to require trial under the circumstances would be "a denial of due process of law." My last statement struck a nerve. The old judge looked down at me and said: "How long have you been out of law school?" I stammered and then fibbed a little bit: "About five years your honor." He then said: "I thought so. Objection overruled."

My colloquy with the judge was the lead story that evening on the front page of the pink sheet of the *Milwaukee Journal*. The events that followed were exciting, to say the least. We decided to prepare and obtain, if we could, a writ of prohibition against the judge to stop the trial. It was in the middle of summer and the Supreme Court was in adjournment. My senior partner called the Chief Justice to see if we could get a hearing at 9:00 the next morning. He said that he would go to trial and see if we could delay the proceedings until we returned from the Supreme Court in Madison. We recruited two shifts of secretaries at the firm to work from six to midnight and from midnight to six. Each of the lawyers for the defendants drafted a long affidavit for officers of their companies and the City to sign setting out in detail the resulting prejudice to our clients if the trial were to proceed without further preparation. I well remember taking the affidavit out to the home of the Schlitz vice president to have it executed. I caught him at a dinner party where he was entertaining several guests at pool side. The lawyer for A.O. Smith and I were given the task of preparing the writ. We detailed the facts and wrote and rewrote a brief on the law. By 4:30 that next morning, we had completed a one hundred and twenty page document.

After breakfast, we left for Madison, ninety miles away, to have a hearing before the Supreme Court. At 9:00 a.m., we were ushered into the Supreme Court conference chamber where four other justices along with the Chief Justice had informally convened to hear us. We presented our lengthy petition for a writ of prohibition and then, at the request of the court, summarized its contents. After the justices asked certain questions, we were asked to leave the room so that they could confer. In about ten minutes time, we were called back to find that each of the justices had signed our prepared order granting us a writ of prohibition enjoining the trial judge from trying the case at the scheduled time and removing the judge from further proceedings.

At this point, the clerk interrupted the proceedings to say that I had an emergency phone call from my firm. I was excused. Grubb was calling from the courthouse in Milwaukee to say that the trial judge had announced to all of the parties and their counsel that he had decided to continue the trial on his own motion and to recuse himself from further proceedings. I immediately returned to the conference chambers and gave the news to the Supreme Court Justices. They asked us to adjourn to the corridor. When we were summoned back, the signed order granting the writ had been shredded and removed from the pleadings. The Chief Justice announced that based on the phone call, the Court felt that the matter had been mooted. The Chief Justice asked each of us to keep the matter confidential. We returned to Milwaukee, tired but extremely satisfied that our hard work had paid off.

The Dishonest Judge

Every once in a while you read about a dishonest judge. Perhaps the most well known incident concerns Judge Manton of the Second Circuit who in the late 1920's took bribes and payoffs for several favors and rulings in bankruptcy proceedings. Similarly, when Senator Joe McCarthy was serving as a Wisconsin Circuit Judge in the 1930's, he directed his court reporter to destroy the transcript of a trial involving a friend of his who had been sued by the State Dairy Commission for charging excessive rates for dairy products. McCarthy had ruled for a friend and allegedly to prevent the state from appealing the ruling, he had ordered the transcript destroyed. I have never personally encountered a dishonest judge. The closest I came to such a situation was when a trial judge tried to help my opponent who had missed a jurisdictional deadline for an appeal. The judge backdated the pleading. I discovered it because I had checked at the clerk's office and found that the appeal had not been timely filed. I was terribly frustrated because I did not want to publicly embarrass the judge. Yet, in representing my client, I had resolved that I had to raise the jurisdictional issue on appeal and challenge the filing. A few days later, opposing counsel called and told me what had happened. He told me he had not slept for over two nights because of what the judge had done. He paid $10,000, the amount of the verdict. He paid the verdict from the law firm money and told his client that he had been delinquent in not getting the notice filed on time. Whatever happens, the lawyer must act to ensure that his client's interests prevail and no wrongful complicity by a judge should ever prevent the lawyer from doing what is right.

THE JUDGE AS A FACT FINDER

One question counsel often faces is whether to try the case before a judge or a jury. Within our judicial system, the judge is deemed, at least as a matter of law, just as fair as a jury in determining the facts. However, the lawyer must determine whether, under the circumstances of the case, it is better to try the case before a single judge or a group of jurors. Much to the chagrin of trial judges, my answer has always been that it is better to try a case before a six or twelve person jury. I do not say this in denigration of the trial judge. However a judge is no more an expert in finding facts than any other citizen. In other words there is always safety in numbers. I would rather have two or more persons decide the facts than one. The single judge is trained in the law, but factual determinations rest so much more on the background and experience of the fact finder. Under the circumstances I think it is better to submit contested facts to a group rather than to a single person. If a judge is prejudiced one way or the other, there is no one else to point out the error of his way. Furthermore, a judge is trained in the law and knowing the law can easily cause him or her to become more result-oriented in finding crucial facts for or against you. Finally, many judges see and hear so many witnesses I think they are more prone to stereotype certain witnesses, particularly expert witnesses, and either reject them outright or accept what they may say without qualifications.

CHAPTER VI
THE JURY

THE VALUE OF A JURY

BLUE RIBBON JURIES

SELECTING THE JURY
Hiring Jury Experts
Lawyer Voir Dire
Achieving Rapport
Lawyers Can Note Weakness Of Case
Challenges For Cause
Peremptory Challenge

DO NOT ATTEMPT TO CURRY FAVOR OF THE JURY
The Overly Solicitous Lawyer
Watch Out For Your Opponent

PREJUDICING THE JURY—THE WRONG WAY
Silver Bell Mine Trial
Caution Others Not To Mix With The Jury

JUROR RESENTMENT
Keeping Notes
During The Trial, Watch Out For Possible Juror Prejudice.
The Jury And The Final Argument
Visiting The Scene
Jurors As Witnesses
Juror Questions

SIZE OF JURY

CONCLUSION

THE VALUE OF A JURY

The fundamental value of a jury is that it represents a body of citizens drawn from a cross section of the community. As is often recognized, a jury brings the composite mores of the community to the resolution of factual disputes. A jury possesses a sense of community fairness. The best characterization as to the quality of a jury and its function was written by Justice Hunt in *Sioux City & Pacific R. Co. v. Stout*, 84 U.S. 657, 664 (1874) when he said:

> ". . . Twelve [persons] of the average of the community, comprising [persons] of education and [persons] of little education, [persons] of learning and [persons] whose learning consists only in what they have themselves seen and heard, the merchant, the mechanic, the farmer, the laborer; these sit together, consult, apply their separate experience of the affairs of life to the facts proven, and draw a unanimous conclusion. This average judgment thus given it is the great effort of the law to obtain. It is assumed that twelve [persons] know more of the common affairs of life than does one [person], that they can draw wiser and safer conclusions from admitted facts thus occurring than can a single judge."

When the media (television or newspapers) attempt to exploit the spectacular in celebrated trials, many individuals feel that a more just result can be obtained by submitting criminal cases to a panel of "educated" judges rather than to a jury of lay people. This would be a tragic mistake. Our citizens should never forfeit one of their most precious rights—that of deciding the rights and obligations of other citizens—to officials of the government. The lessons to be gained from the trials of the Nazi judges at Nuremburg, who had followed the dictates of their political leaders, rather than the law, should never be forgotten. Power can corrupt. Judges may have expertise in determining the law, but they do not have a superior sense of fairness over other citizens.

Judges often possess as much, or more, bias than other citizens. It isn't a question of whether judges will try to be fair; the more fundamental question is whether pre-conceived ideas will influence them as much or more than any other citizen. Judges often form stereotyped opinions about certain witnesses. This is especially true of expert witnesses such as doctors or engineers. Some judges favor police officers; some dislike them. Over the years, judges who have heard many cases form preconceived opinions about certain civil or criminal trials. Many judges become "law and order" jurists. A state judge once told me that persons charged with crime "are not people, they are just numbers." As earlier mentioned, another federal trial judge in front of a jury commented: "The government never lies." How would you like to have twelve persons determine your guilt or innocence, if you were charged with a crime, with judges sitting as jurors with a similar frame of mind?

We once heard an appeal in which the trial judge, after jurors rendered a guilty verdict, told the jurors that the government brings only thoroughly investigated, error free cases to trial.

I responded in the appellate opinion as follows:

> "Counsel has called our attention to these comments. Because these remarks were made after the verdict, they concededly cannot be deemed prejudicial; however, they do indirectly reveal the judge's feelings throughout the trial. The trial judge's attitude may have unconsciously driven him to assume a prosecutorial role in the trial, a role which destroyed fair process for the accused.

> We also call attention to these remarks after the verdict under this court's general supervisory capacity over the trial courts. The likelihood that several of the jurors in this case would sit on additional federal criminal cases following this trial is obvious. These comments by the trial judge are clearly prejudicial to the trial of others charged in federal court. Whether the remarks result in actual prejudice can only be determined by the state of mind of each individual juror. We request district court judges not to make such comments; their import obviously diminishes the presumption of innocence of any accused tried in federal court. We deem such remarks to be inaccurate and irrelevant in the trials of criminal defendants in federal court. *United States v. Bland*, 697 F.2d 262 (8th Cir. 1983).

Many well-meaning individuals have difficulty with juries in criminal cases. From the media and television, citizens form their own conclusions as to whether a defendant is guilty or innocent. They do so without the benefit of observing witnesses first hand and without the court's instructions. More important, skepticism in juries, particularly in criminal cases, overlook that our entire criminal justice system is biased in favor of a defendant. The presumption of innocence of any person charged with a crime places the burden of proof on the government to prove guilt beyond a reasonable doubt. Abuse of interrogation outside the courtroom has provided protections to every individual the right not to incriminate themselves and to have the right to effective assistance of counsel. The very requirement of unanimous juries favors the defendant. Some citizens question these principles (that is, until they or their relatives or friends face criminal charges). The history of our forefathers and our own empirical judgment places high value on our liberty and the right to live, and we, as a people, protect all citizens from abuse of power. This is really what our jury system is all about.

Justice Frankfurter once observed that jurors are not so "stupid" that they cannot see "the drift of the evidence." *United States v. Johnson*, 319 U.S. 503, 519 (1943).

My experience as a lawyer and judge has made me a strong advocate for the jury system.

BLUE RIBBON JURIES

Years ago the federal courts utilized what was known as a key man system in calling citizens to serve on juries. This system allowed the clerk of court to call twenty-five or more leading citizens of the state, such as bankers, heads of industry, physicians, presidents of corporations, and the like, and request they suggest the names of their acquaintances to be placed on the jury selection list. Federal court juries utilized a great many reputable farmers, businessmen, school teachers, and corporate executives on juries. There were few members of the working class, few laborers and no unemployed people. There were few minorities on the list. These were called "blue ribbon juries." In the state courts the juries were markedly different. State juries were typically chosen from voter registration lists, telephone books and the like. Ordinary citizens from all walks of life served on state juries. It always was astonishing to me that it was not until as late as the 1960s that the elitism of federal juries was changed. Courts surprisingly had given lip service upholding the constitutionality of the key man system. Finally, because there was so much clamor for change, Congress altered the whole process and eliminated the key man system.

Before passage of the "new" jury law in 1967, I was privileged to testify before the Senate Judiciary Committee and observed in my testimony:

> I have been alarmed over the past several years at the continued complaints of some trial lawyers regarding the selection of federal juries by the key man system.

> A lawyer from Kansas tells me his firm avoids federal court litigation because only the people from white collared positions are selected to serve. He says that he represents working people and they are subtly excluded from the jury array before it comes to the Court House.

> A criminal trial lawyer from St. Louis says that most of his clients are poor people and he dreads trying cases before federal juries. He feels the class structure of the federal jury is such that it is not representative since persons who have similar economic backgrounds of clients are not on the jury.

> A trial lawyer from Minnesota says that his choice of selection has been narrowed on a federal jury since the working man was seldom on the panel.

SELECTING THE JURY

Undoubtedly, a lawyer's understanding of human relationships is more essential in selecting a jury than in any other area of law. For the most part, law and legal principles are out the window, and human psychology takes over. Contrary to popular belief, choosing a jury does not turn on selecting jurors who will be favorable to your case, but in eliminating jurors who might be unfavorable to your side. It is easier to discover a juror's possible bias and prejudice against your client than it is to find someone who will surely vote for your side. The idea of selecting a juror is to find someone who will be fair in hearing your case rather than someone who is prejudiced for your case. If counsel keeps this simple principle in mind, the selection of a jury will take on a different focus.

The jury selection process in both federal and state courts has three primary components: The voir dire, where the judge, and more often the lawyers, question prospective jurors to determine their fitness and appropriateness to serve on a particular case; strikes for cause, when the judge removes potential jurors from the panel for bias or other factors making them incompetent to serve; and preemptory strikes, when the lawyers may disqualify jurors whom they believe may be unfair to their client. In recent years, the concept of the preemptory strike has come under attack. Many people, unwisely I believe, feel the preemptory strike allows lawyers too much leeway in selecting or rejecting certain ethnic persons so as to create a bias jury.

Hiring Jury Experts

In complicated trials, especially when there are large sums at stake, or when a criminal defendant is well funded, lawyers sometimes hire psychologists or other professionals to help select jurors. My friend, Brian O'Neill, who successfully tried the punitive damages case against Exxon for Alaska fishermen, told me the plaintiffs spent more than $250,000 hiring experts to help them choose a jury to decide the Valdez oil spill case. In the spectacle of O.J. Simpson's murder trial, experts prepared 228 questions for the lawyers to consider when selecting jurors. This approach may be fine if the client has the money to pay for the process. The theory is that so much is at stake that it makes sense to go all out to achieve the right result. However, I have known trials where despite the expenditure of large sums on jury specialists, the jury returned an adverse verdict. I personally question the value of "jury experts;" they attempt to manipulate the jury system by selecting jurors biased toward one side. More often than not, this will backfire.

In any event, in the ordinary jury trial, the client does not have the funds to go to such extremes. The lawyer is left to his or her own devices. It may sound trite, but the best tool any lawyer possesses under these circumstances is the exercise of common sense and basic intuition about people. Many books have been written about the tactics and strategies of choosing a jury. Some lawyers have even recommended judging prospective jurors by their nationality (for example, Clarence Darrow once wrote that a person of German or Swedish descent might be bullheaded or stubborn). Many lawyers feel the most salient measures are a juror's employment or family background, (for example, a wife of a physician or a nurse might minimize a plaintiff's complaint of injury, or a truck driver might be more sympathetic to another truck driver or, depending on the case, perhaps be more critical). In trying injury cases in rural areas, one quickly learns that farm families endure accidents that go unreported and uncompensated. As a result, persons growing up on the farm are generally not sympathetic in awarding damages for someone else's injuries.

There is another basic rule I always followed: Never allow a lawyer to sit on the jury. The same applies to the lawyer's spouse. Lay jurors will always look to the lawyer for direction. Notwithstanding the judge's instructions on the law, there is always grave danger that most of the jurors will turn to the lawyer-juror to explain the law. Such a jury can quickly become a one-person jury.

No simple rule of thumb governs every situation. Counsel needs effective insight into a prospective juror's sense of fairness or bias. The more experience counsel has selecting jurors the more efficient and confident he or she will be using judgment in this very important process.

Lawyer Voir Dire

Every jurisdiction has its rules about selecting the jury. Most states allow the lawyers to conduct the *voir dire*, that is questioning of prospective jurors in advance of selection. Most federal courts, however, will not allow the lawyers to ask the jurors questions, but require counsel to submit written questions that the judge will ask. This practice is condoned in the name of expediency on the theory that lawyers take too much time asking questions.

In my judgment, it is wrong to refuse to allow lawyers to *voir dire* prospective jurors. Judges can control abuse of *voir dire* by the lawyers just as they control abuse in argument or in the examination of witnesses. Each lawyer should be allowed to see how individual jurors react to the lawyer and the lawyer's questions. I always said before an airline pilot takes off, the pilot wants to know what the weather may be once he is in the air. A judge does not know the lawyer's case other than by the pleadings. Jurors often are nonresponsive to questions that the judge might pose, especially if the court's inquiry requires a simple show of hands for a response. Many judges ask the abstract question: "Can you be fair?" I have never observed any juror who will not raise their hand to show an affirmative response to that question.

When questioned by a lawyer, however, I have observed jurors look away or sit up straight in their chairs even in response to neutral questions. This is a strong sign of bias against the lawyer's case. For example, in a case I handled as a trial judge, I asked each prospective juror whether their prior jury service would create any bias or prejudice to any of the parties. Each juror said, "No." When I allowed counsel to question the jurors, one responded to the plaintiff's counsel that she served on a case in which the lawyer asked for too much money. She then inquired, "How much are your asking for?" The lawyer was careful to respond that the court would instruct the jury about damages, and that the plaintiff was asking only for that amount of money which would reasonably compensate her for her injuries. The lawyer was also wise in striking the juror with a preemptory strike. The court's questioning alone did not develop the possible antagonism the juror obviously possessed against a personal injury claimant.

Chief Justice Burger was the guiding force to reduce federal civil juries from twelve to six. The argument was made that the six person jury would be more economic and more efficient. There is now a movement to return to the twelve person jury. He also was a strong advocate to eliminate *voir dire* by either judges or lawyers. He felt that lawyer *voir dire* caused excessive delay. He once announced to all the Chief Circuit Judges that he had observed a jury selected to serve in a criminal trial in England. He said there was no *voir dire*. The clerk simply called twelve persons into the box. The barristers were given a background list, age, employment, nationality, etc. to study. Each juror was then asked to stand and repeat their oath. He observed that the system was foolproof because one woman called could not speak or understand English and when she was asked to give her oath, the court discovered that she could not speak English "and they struck" her right away. He suggested that we each go back to our circuits and recommend to all district judges to adopt such a system. No one took him seriously.

I recall a case I tried in federal court in which my client was an illiterate Mexican laborer who lost his thumb on a railroad boxcar while loading produce. My client's orthopedic surgeon testified that the plaintiff was totally disabled because he was fit only to work as a laborer. With the loss of his thumb, he could not hold a shovel or use his hand to pick up heavy objects. I submitted a written question to be asked by the court: "Would any juror be prejudiced against the plaintiff because he is an itinerant Mexican laborer?" The jurors, of course, all raised their hands indicating they would not be prejudiced. I had no opportunity to question the jurors personally.

The jury awarded only $10,000 even though we presented evidence of substantially greater damages. After the trial, two of the jurors told me exactly this: "The plaintiff is just an itinerant Mexican laborer and we did not feel he should get as much as any American laborer with the same injury." If I had been permitted to question these jurors during voir dire, I might have discovered this bias. Since this was in federal court, I did not have the opportunity.

Achieving Rapport

It is imperative that attorneys attempt to achieve as much rapport as they can with the jurors if, and when, they are allowed to conduct jury examination in voir dire. This means you should be fair and courteous in the examination. You should never be argumentative. An experienced trial lawyer taught me to memorize the names of the prospective jurors and their occupations as they are called to sit in the jury box. This allows counsel to question each juror without notes, and to converse with them in a friendly and informal manner. It is worth the effort to memorize the juror's names even when the prospective panel has 18 or more members. As defense counsel, I always had more time to memorize the names of the jurors because the plaintiff's counsel questioned the jurors first. However, after a short time, I was able to memorize the names even when I served as the plaintiff's counsel. I never tried a jury case where one or more jurors didn't ask me after the verdict how I was able to remember all of their names and occupations. They always stated they were impressed with my informality and relaxed manner of the pretrial questioning.

Lawyers have a golden opportunity to impress jurors. If jurors feel you have legal skills and are fair in your approach to the case, they might call you later to represent them or members of their family. I tried cases long before the Supreme Court held that lawyers could advertise (thank goodness!). Clients were largely dependent upon reputation in the community for selecting lawyers. I always derived great satisfaction when former jurors would ask me to represent them when they were confronted with the need for legal services.

Lawyers Can Note Weakness Of Case

In approaching the selection of jurors, it is wise to examine the weakness of your case and to consider collateral factors that should be examined when selecting jurors. For example, if you are trying a case that involves a particular statute, rule or regulation, you should ask prospective jurors whether they have encountered the rule or statute. If your case involves a passenger suing the driver of a car, for example, you should find out whether jurors would disagree with a law that allows the passengers to sue the host drivers. I handled many such cases. One time a one juror responded that she felt that it would be poor sportsmanship to allow the guest to sue the host. The judge ultimately excused the juror for cause. I then asked if anyone else felt the same way. One woman juror raised her hand and said: "I think it would be poor sportsmanship if you sued for more than the insurance policy." I gulped. I said I would prefer the judge answer her inquiry. The judge proceeded to say that insurance was not involved in the case. Perhaps I took unfair advantage of the juror's question. In final argument, I told the jury that we had sued for $25,000 but my client wanted to be a good sport, and was asking for only $10,000. The jury verdict was $10,000.

If your client had stopped for a beer before the accident, it is much better to bring this out in voir dire than to have your opponent bring it out during his examination.

Challenges For Cause

To be successfully challenged for cause, the juror has to be legally disqualified or admit to bias. Jurors may express doubt about your case, but affirm that they can listen to all of the evidence and be fair. If you can question a problematic juror in such a way to get her to remove herself from the case for cause, you will save one of your scarce preemptory challenges for some other juror who concerns you. For example, assume that Mrs. Jones questions the law that allows a guest passenger to sue her host, yet affirms her willingness to decide the case solely on the evidence and the law of the case. Having asked her about her concerns about the law, you follow up: "Mrs. Jones, if you were the plaintiff in this case, and as a passenger you were claiming injury because of the driver's alleged negligence, would you feel comfortable in having twelve people with the feeling you have expressed sitting on the jury to decide your case?" "Well, probably not." "Then would you feel better in not sitting on this case?" "Probably." "I will then ask the judge to excuse you." If the judge does not, you undoubtedly will need to exercise your preemptory challenge. Counsel cannot allow her to serve on the jury.

Peremptory Challenge

While challenges for cause must be ruled on by the court in the past, the exercise of preemptory challenge has generally been exclusively within the discretion of the lawyer. Recent Supreme Court cases have now subjected that discretion to legal and constitutional scrutiny when race or gender is involved. Preemptory challenges are very important. It is here where the lawyer must use his or her best judgment in deciding who to eliminate from the ultimate jury panel. As I have previously stated, there has been growing criticism with preemptory challenges as the lawyer may exercise objections over who will sit on the jury. However, I find it difficult to believe that lawyers should not be able to disqualify individuals who lend an appearance of prejudice to their client's case. I make this observation with balanced qualification; lawyers must weigh their strikes within constitutional limits to avoid intrusion into gender/race concerns. Both sides participate in jury selection the same way. So, the use of preemptory challenges does not favor one side over the other.

DO NOT ATTEMPT TO CURRY FAVOR OF THE JURY

The Overly Solicitous Lawyer

Trial judges usually instruct juries at the beginning of the trial to avoid discussing the case except during their deliberations. Of course, this includes the lawyers who are trying the case. When sitting as a trial judge, I always tell the jurors they should have no contact with any of the lawyers and they should understand that the lawyers are not being rude to them by not addressing them or even saying good morning to them. If they happen to run into one of the lawyers at lunch or in the hall they should know that I have asked the lawyers not to engage even in social amenities with them. If the lawyers or for that matter anyone else attempts to contact them, they should report it to me, the trial judge. Some judges may think that telling the lawyers not to exchange social amenities with the jury is carrying it too far, but I use that instruction more to protect the lawyer and his or her client's case than anything else. I have had several experiences that persuaded me of the merits of doing so.

DO NOT ATTEMPT TO CURRY FAVOR OF THE JURY

One time a lawyer defending a case for a railroad stood at the entry of the courtroom every morning and afternoon. He held the door open for each of the jurors and was always solicitous to each one of them they would come or go. He would often greet them by name and in syrupy voice say " good morning, Mrs. Smith" or "So nice to see you again, Mr. Jones." On the last day of the trial it had rained during the noon recess; many of the jurors had been rained on. The lawyer stood at the door and apologized to each one of them for having gotten wet. During oral argument he brought it up again and told them how sorry he was they had been rained on and how this was beyond the call of duty of a juror. To me his conduct was sickening and improper.

I had avoided contact with the jurors, but I did not want to make an issue of counsel's conduct because I was not certain how the jury was reacting to it. After the case was over, a friend told me that a secretary at his company had been on the jury. He told me that the juror told people at the company that one juror announced at the beginning of deliberations that she wanted everyone to know that regardless of their feelings she was not going to vote in favor of the railroad attorney because "his tactics made her sick." Several of the other jurors agreed. We obtained a substantial verdict against the railroad.

Watch Out For Your Opponent

I have observed lawyers attempt to influence jurors by questionable, but lawful means. I recall a case where an orthopedic doctor was being sued for malpractice. The defense circulated the list of jurors to all the orthopedic doctors in the city. Every doctor who had treated any member of the jury or the family of the juror visited the courtroom during the trial and saw fit, just before the testimony would commence or after it was over, to go forward and shake hands with the doctor defendant. The jury could observe their friendship.

In another case I tried, I observed on the second day of the trial that the claims manager of the insurer was visiting court and making obvious efforts to be seen consulting with the defense counsel and his client. This was his right, but I felt it was unusual. I became suspicious. Why would the claims manager be in court? I requested a hearing before the judge. I asked if the claims manager knew anyone on the jury. Counsel stammered that he did not know. I asked the judge if we could inquire of the claims manager if he knew anyone on the jury in the court's presence. The court granted my motion. The claims manager admitted that he did know one of the jurors on the panel, but he said he was present in court simply because he was interested in the trial. He added that he had not talked to the juror about the case. I told the judge of the frequent consultations with defense counsel and his client. I stated: "Judge, I want him out of here." Defense counsel did not oppose my motion. Watch out for such maneuvers!

PREJUDICING THE JURY—THE WRONG WAY

Silver Bell Mine Trial

One of the most bizarre jury trials in which I participated occurred in Milwaukee in the mid 1950's. The case taught me that jurors are very perceptive of a lawyer's prejudicial conduct.

In this case, our firm represented a group of individuals who had invested in a uranium mine in Colorado, called the Silver Bell Mine. With the advent of nuclear power, many groups were exploring for uranium, almost like the Gold Rush 100 years before. In 1953, the five original investors incorporated a mining company that would carry out the exploration. Among the original investors, it was agreed that each investor would have an option to purchase up to 100,000 additional shares for $1 a share. The by-laws provided that each investor was required to exercise his option by midnight December 31, 1953.

Four of the five investors timely exercised their option before December 31, 1953. The only one of the original investors who did not exercise his option was a surgeon who lived in Milwaukee. I shall call him Dr. Brown (not his real name). In the spring of 1954, the stock rose 3 1/4 per share. Shortly before the SEC ordered, pending further investigation, all trading of the stock to cease, the company received a registered letter from Dr. Brown stating that on December 30, 1953 he had forwarded a timely exercise of his option to purchase the additional 100,000 shares at $1 a share. Dr. Brown attached a carbon copy of the purported December 30 letter. The company, however, had never received Dr. Brown's letter exercising the option. It refused to honor the exercise of his untimely option. Dr. Brown then sued the company and the other investors for $500,000.

My ultimate success in defending the case was not attributable to any trial proficiency I may have learned in my early years out of law school. Dr. Brown's claim was clearly fraudulent. He relied solely upon his testimony without corroboration. Dr. Brown testified he typed the December 30 letter himself (even though his secretary always typed all other correspondence, including the later registered letter.) And, even though the original letter exercising the stock option was a crucial document, he allegedly sent it by regular mail and did not follow up to verify its arrival for months.

Dr. Brown testified at trial that he had initially delayed exercising his option because the other investors had told him the mine was a failure. On cross-examination, he conceded that he had overlooked a letter which he had written long hand to the president of the company (our client) in the fall of 1953 stating he was *not* going to exercise his option because he had visited the mine and he was satisfied it had no uranium. The jury was not out long. By special interrogatory, it answered that Dr. Brown never exercised his option (thus there was no liability).

The facts of this unusual case only shade the background of the almost incredible events that occurred during the trial. The attorney representing Dr. Brown stands out as the most absurd and most incredulous lawyer I have ever met.

For sake of complete anonymity, I shall call Dr. Brown's lawyer "Attorney. X." During my opening statement, X began a series of unbelievable tactics which continued throughout the trial. As I cross-examined the plaintiff's witnesses, X began to rip off blank sheets of paper from yellow legal pads and crumple them up. It became obvious that he did wish the jury to hear my questions or the answers. Periodically he would rise and walk the length of the room to the water cooler, clicking the metal cleats on the sole of his shoes. He would rattle and shake the cooler to cause further distraction. I noticed as well that X from time to time would actually wink at certain members of the jury.

After three days of this, I finally asked for a hearing outside the presence of the jury. I explained to the very capable trial judge, that I simply did not know what was going on. Did X know some of the jurors? Was he winking at friends on the jury? The judge asked: "Why the winking?" X actually shook his fist at the judge and said that he had every right to use whatever trial tactics he thought were effective, and the court did not have the right to restrict him in carrying out his trial strategy. The court assured X that he was "wrong." The judge said his behavior amounted to misconduct and that in the court's judgment it was prejudicing X's own client. The court said if his unusual behavior continued he would consider granting a mistrial to protect X's client. The trial had gone along far enough that I was satisfied that the last thing we wanted was a mistrial.

The next day I was cross-examining the plaintiff, Dr. Brown. The judge interrupted and stated that he wished to excuse the jury in order to talk to counsel outside its presence. The court then turned to X and said he noticed X was continuing his rude and bewildering tactics, but more importantly he was still winking at the jury. He said he must now give serious consideration to granting a mistrial. The judge said this was his last warning to X and recalled the jury.

One of my clients who was an original investor and promoter of the mining company was a huge Irishman who weighed approximately 275 pounds. I will call him O'Toole. The night before I was prepared to rest the case for the defense, the headline of the Milwaukee paper read that my client, O'Toole, had been indicted by the federal government for income tax fraud. I decided not to use him as a defense witness because I was afraid of calling undue attention to him. After all, he was accused of fraud in this case also. I thought the less notice of O'Toole by the jury the better.

We somehow had survived to final argument. X had continued his disturbances and continued winking at the jury. I did not object further to X's misconduct because I did not want a mistrial.

I was midway through final argument with my back to X and my clients when I heard this loud movement at the counsel's table. I turned and saw O'Toole had risen from his chair. He yelled: "Your Honor, X is winking at the jury again!" Although the jury had been excused during the judge's warnings to X, our clients, including O'Toole, had been present.

Another recess occurred. This time I had to beg the court not to declare a mistrial. Fortunately, he did not. ·

There is more. Before the case went to the jury, I was cross-examining Dr. Brown one morning at about 11:00 when I began to question him about the incriminating letter he wrote stating his intention to decline the option. X had never seen the letter. His client did not tell his own lawyer about it. After X read the letter, he turned to the court and in what turned out to be a complete fabrication, stated: "Your Honor, could Dr. Brown please be excused from the witness stand? He has a major operation to perform at the hospital at 11:45 a.m. and must leave immediately." I was not about to make objection, although I sincerely doubted the veracity of X's statement. The court reluctantly granted X's request if he assured the court Brown could return to the witness stand by 2:00 that afternoon.

The trial continued without Dr. Brown. After five minutes, I turned around and there in the hallway peering through a window was none other than Dr. Brown. He remained there until the noon recess. When he returned in the afternoon, he admitted he had written the letter but testified he had changed his mind about exercising the option to purchase the stock.

During final argument I called attention to Dr. Brown's strange recusal and Attorney X's purported reason for his leaving. I was in the courtroom when the verdict was returned. Afterwards, one of the jurors approached me and said: "We want to compliment you in the manner in which you tried your case. However, we did not appreciate when you pointed out that Dr. Brown went out in the hallway, peering into the window, while he supposedly was in surgery. You did not give us credit for sufficient intelligence for observing what happened." I asked some of the jurors why they had answered the special interrogatory on damages contained in the verdict form, by awarding the plaintiff damages for the full value of the stock as of the date Dr. Brown allegedly had exercised his option. This surprised me. I thought we had demonstrated that the stock was actually worthless because no uranium was found. The jurors answered that they knew that Dr. Brown would not win because they found he had not exercised his option. Therefore they wanted to set the damages as high as possible so that Dr. Brown and his lawyer would feel as bad as possible in losing the case.

I have never forgotten that. Never underestimate the intelligence and common sense of the jury. The recollection of these events serves only to demonstrate the folly of the lawyer who feels he or she may win cases by currying favor with the jury. After reading this account, one may say that no lawyer would ever act as I have described. I concede that this lawyer stands alone, but I have observed other lawyers attempting to curry favor with juries in only slightly less outrageous fashion. Such tactics always backfire.

Caution Others Not To Mix With The Jury

Trial judges frequently admonish the parties not to have contact with jurors, but rarely do they separately admonish witnesses. I have been in trials where witnesses waiting to be called to the stand enter into innocent conversations with jurors without anyone knowing that this is wrong. The problem is that when the witness takes the stand, that juror can relate to the witness as a "nice person," or perhaps as someone that was secretly trying to curry the jury's favor. Lawyers should tell not only their clients to avoid contact with jurors outside the courtroom at all costs, but they should also admonish their clients' families and friends, all witnesses, and anyone else connected to the proceedings.

One time I was sitting as a trial judge when an attractive female juror wrote me a note asking to see me as soon as possible. I called a recess. She brought two additional jurors with her. The three jurors told me that from the beginning of the trial a man sitting in the audience had been staring at the female juror. She said at first she thought it her imagination but now realized that he never looked at any of the witnesses while they testified. He just stared at her. She was scared.

I told them that I had not noticed, but that I would immediately take care of the situation. I called the lawyers into chambers outside of her presence. The individual was identified as the Claims Manager for the defendant company. The defense lawyer said that there had to be some mistake. I directed the lawyer to tell the individual to leave the court room and the court house. I felt the defendant might well be prejudiced if the individual remained where the jurors would observe him talking to the defense team. The problem was that the claims manager had been sitting on the plaintiff's side of the aisle with all of the plaintiff's witnesses. The plaintiff was concerned that the jurors would associate the individual with his side. I then called the three jurors back into chambers and told them that the individual had been asked to leave; that he was not involved in the *trial* of the lawsuit and that the jurors should disregard the incident. I asked, on the record, whether this had prejudiced the female juror in any way against either the plaintiff or the defendant. She answered that it had not. The jury returned a very large verdict for the plaintiff. I will always wonder if the jurors knew the individual was associated with the defendant.

JUROR RESENTMENT

Keeping Notes

Different jurisdictions have different rules about whether jurors are allowed to take notes. Some jurisdictions leave this question to the discretion of the trial judge. Strong arguments can be made in favor of note taking. I believe that note taking helps jurors remember the testimony. The general objection and the prevailing view appears to be that note takers are not always accurate. The concern is that jurors confused about a fact might be more apt to believe someone's notes, even if wrong, rather than their own memory.

If you try a case in a jurisdiction where note taking is proscribed, be careful how you make an objection. I recall a juror taking notes during the testimony of our chief witness in a complicated civil trial. I notice her note taking, but I felt the juror's reaction to other testimony suggested she was favorable to our case. I did not object. Counsel for the defendant noticed, paused and asked permission to approach the bench. At the bench he whispered to the trial judge that juror No. 12 was taking notes in violation of state law. The court then turned to the jury and stated, "It has been called to my attention that one or more of you are taking notes. I cautioned you in the beginning of the trial that this was not proper under state law. Therefore, if any of you have notes, I would respectfully ask you to destroy those notes at this time." Juror No. 12 turned her chair to face defense counsel, held her notes high in both hands and proceeded to tear them up in a contemptuous disdain of defense counsel's motion. At this point, counsel approached the bench and moved for a mistrial on the ground of prejudice. The court overruled the motion. As defense counsel returned to his seat, juror No. 12 turned her chair to face away from counsel. I knew we had at least one juror on our side.

During The Trial, Watch Out For Possible Juror Prejudice

Events can occur during the course of trial that may inappropriately influence jurors. In the course of a two week trial, one juror requested a private audience with the court. She told the court she was having company the next day and wanted to be excused. The court had asked jurors during voir dire whether they could sit for at least ten days without inconvenience or conflict. No one had indicated a problem. The court refused to excuse the juror. The court then told both counsel of his conversation with the juror. He stated the juror was very angry. Fortunately, the next day we reached a settlement. Both counsel were in court when the jury was told of the settlement and the jurors were dismissed. The woman approached me as they left the courtroom. She said: "It is a good thing you settled!" I politely said: "I don't understand. We did not object to you being excused." She replied: "You brought the law suit. I wouldn't be here if it wasn't for you."

I recalled that case recently when reviewing a criminal conviction in which a juror received an anonymous call stating: "We know where you live." The juror was scared. She asked to be excused. The trial judge consulted with counsel and stated that he would excuse the juror, who naturally blamed the defendant. The defense denied any knowledge of the call. Defense counsel requested that the juror be asked whether she had told the other jurors. She had. Defense counsel requested that the judge hold a hearing to question the other jurors. The judge refused on the ground that the call had been made to the excused juror and did not affect the rest of the jurors. On appeal, we reversed and remanded and stated that the trial judge must always act diligently to preserve a defendant's constitutional right to a fair trial. The trial court was directed to hold a hearing to "determine whether other jurors who knew of the threat were able to act impartially and without bias."

The Jury And The Final Argument

Many lawyers underestimate jury negative reaction that results from even subtle but overt attempts to prejudice the jury through final argument. My experience has taught me that the most effective final argument by counsel is a straight forward summation of facts which should be persuasive to the jury. Attempts to disparage opposing counsel or to attack by vindictive name-calling opposing witnesses may often boomerang. Once a lawyer in closing argument attempted to belittle two nice middle-aged housewives, who were witnesses to an accident. Opposing counsel had tried several criminal cases. As I earlier related in summation, he told the jury that no one could believe the "two floozies" we had called. The jurors deeply resented it. On another occasion, I called an African-American woman as a witness. Opposing counsel, argued that the only reason I had called the witness was an attempt to curry favor with the two blacks on the jury. After we received a favorable verdict, I visited with other members of the jury. They told me that the entire jury felt opposing counsel was "out of line."

Perhaps some lawyers have the ability to tell stories or read poetry to a jury without appearing to be corny. I think most jurors are not swayed by flowery talk unconnected to the case.

I once tried a case against two old time trial lawyers when, just before I started final argument, my mentor gave me a note. He said the plaintiff's lawyer arguing on rebuttal was hard of hearing. He noted the lawyer always closed his final summation with a corny poem. My mentor suggested that I lower my voice and tell the jury that my opponent would attempt to influence them by using a little verse in his closing lines. I quietly repeated the verse. I then told the jury they should decide the case on the evidence and not be taken in by an attempt by counsel to create sympathy. Counsel did not hear me. When he argued, true to form, he made an impassioned plea to the jury and then stated in closing he would like to repeat a little poem about justice that he felt was appropriate. I do not remember the exact verse, but it went something like this:

> *Do as wisemen did in days of old*
> *Wisemen, who in ancient Babylon, prayed night and day,*
> *So the ancient story 'tis told.*
> *Seeking heavenly guidance to exalt justice in every way.*

By the time he was finished the entire jury was laughing out loud. Plaintiff's associate counsel turned to my mentor and said: "DeLacy, you S.O.B."

We won. I am confident the poem helped pierce any shred of credibility plaintiff's case may have had.

The moral of the story—be yourself. Don't try to inject, at least superficially, sympathy in any case.

Visiting The Scene

There may be circumstances when it is strategic to request the jury visit the scene of an accident or location where an event took place. Such jury visits are within the discretion of the trial judge. My experience is that counsel should be circumspect about jury visits. There is a great danger that a jury visit will present outside prejudicial factors that neither side or the judge anticipates.

Despite these concerns, I once prevailed upon a trial judge to allow jurors to visit the scene of a key stop sign in an accident case. The stop sign was located on a side road approximately fifty feet from an entrance to the main thoroughfare. Although photographs were admitted into evidence, it was difficult to provide a three dimensional view to demonstrate that the view to the right was completely obstructed at the stop sign.

The plaintiff claimed that he had stopped at the stop sign, looked both to the right and to the left and saw no vehicles approaching. He testified he had a clear view of any vehicles approaching. The plaintiff claimed that our client, the driver of a truck, was speeding when he hit the plaintiff, seriously injuring him. He had been poorly prepared for his deposition. Neither he nor his lawyer had visited the scene of the accident. They had failed to note the obstruction to plaintiff's view of the intersection.

The court granted my motion to take the jury to the scene to view the intersection. We ultimately won a verdict. After the jury returned, the Sheriff, who knew better, told me I owed him a bottle of whiskey. He said that he had driven the jurors to the stop sign and instructed them to be sure to look to the right at the stop sign so they would note the obstructed view. Fortunately he didn't tell my opposing counsel what he had told the jurors.

Jurors As Witnesses

Another problem in having jurors visit the scene is that they become witnesses themselves and can persuade other jurors of their observations. The problem is that sometimes they see things differently than they are. This was brought home to me one time when a juror contrary to the court's instruction, visited the scene of an accident to determine whether a particular witness could see an accident take place. We contended the witness could not see the accident from a window of a farm house.

When the jury retired to the jury room, the juror who visited the scene became witness about what she thought she could observe. She had taken measurements and convinced nine others that she was right. Two jurors dissented. The two jurors called me. They were very angry over the verdict and stated that the juror had convinced the others that our witnesses were wrong. We subpoenaed the juror. She denied that she ever had visited the scene. When I told her that I had the other jurors ready to testify, she said she might have driven by the scene but didn't look. When I asked if she actually had gotten out of her car and taken measurements, she broke down and started to cry. She admitted she had done so. The court gave us a new trial. Whatever goes on in the jury room is usually considered to be inherent in the verdict. However, the verdict may be set aside if external forces play a role in the decision.

Juror Questions

Many trial judges feel that it is useful to allow jurors to ask questions of witnesses. After all, the jurors have the responsibility to determine the facts, so why should they not be able to get their factual questions answered. All this sounds reasonable and perhaps it is. Appellate courts have generally ruled that in the absence of clear prejudice, juror questions lie within the sound discretion of the trial judge. I respectfully disagree with the use of juror questions. Suppose in a criminal case, the juror asks the defendant whether he had ever been arrested before. What happens next? I asked a prosecutor in a criminal appeal what she thought of the idea of allowing jurors to ask questions and she answered that "it was like playing Russian roulette." Should the defendant object? Certainly. In front of the jury?

Trial judges who favor juror questions suggest that to avoid prejudice, the jurors should submit the questions for screening. Such a procedure requires that a juror write out her question and submit it to the judge and the judge then submit it to the lawyers, outside the presence of the jury, I hope, for possible objection. The delay in this procedure could be extremely disruptive if several jurors actively present inquiries. And what happens if the question is improper? The juror is left in a quandary about whom to blame for not having the question answered.

I submit jury questioning tends to usurp the role of a lawyer who knows the rules of evidence and who knows the theoretical balance of what needs to be proven in each phase of the case. How does this affect the rules of cross-examination in terms of opening up collateral matters not otherwise subject to questioning? Much can be written in the ongoing debate about jury questions. I think it sets the stage for possible reversal. If I were a lawyer, I would clear the issue with the trial judge before the case commences and state an early objection.

CHAPTER VI — THE JURY

In one case, *United States v. Johnson*, 892 F.2d 707, 714-15 (8th Cir. 1989), I observed the following in a concurring opinion:

> Counsel's job is to use his knowledge of the case's details and his skills of cross-examination to draw out for the jury potential misperceptions in the witnesses' testimony and weaknesses in the other side's story. To allow the factfinder to join in this exploration encourages it to prematurely adopt the interpretation of one side or the other. In the process of interrogation the jury loses the open-mindedness the process requires them to retain until all the evidence is in and the court's instructions are given. To reach the truth requires skillful advocacy before a neutral factfinder willing to listen to the argument. If the juror begins to match his interrogation skills with the lawyer all of that is lost.
>
> . . . When the jury becomes an advocate or inquisitor in the process, it forsakes its role of arbiter between the government and its citizens. The record in the present case shows that, of the several witnesses who testified, the jurors directed all but one of their questions to the defendant. They asked him why he had arranged the drug sales, whether he had gone to drug treatment, and whether he received money for brokering the transactions. These questions underscore the possibility that if given the chance to aggressively interrogate a defendant, the jury may turn to demanding that the defendant justify himself, rather than waiting for the government to justify its prosecution of him.
>
> Jury interrogation of defendants not only impairs the attainment of just results; it demeans the very appearance of justice. As Justice Frankfurter said about a judge who appeared to take sides in a trial, "[t]hese are subtle matters, for they concern the ingredients of what constitutes justice. Therefore, justice must satisfy the appearance of justice." *Offutt v. Untied States*, 348 U.S. 11, 14 (1954). Because juror questions give the impression that the defendant faces a tribunal biased against him, the moral authority of the court and trial suffers.
>
> Juror interrogation, in either a civil or criminal case, is fraught with danger and borders on a finding of prejudice per se. I express a hope it will cease . . . .

SIZE OF JURY

In all my years of litigation, I only had one hung jury. I represented a black woman whose husband had been killed in an industrial accident. The trial lasted almost three weeks. I heard from several jurors that the only juror that would not vote in favor of the plaintiff was a white laborer, who expressed a deep prejudice against blacks. I will never forget my co-counsel calling me when the judge dismissed the jurors because they could not bring in an unanimous verdict. He said: "Don't feel too badly, Don. Remember that Jesus Christ could not pick twelve of them either."

Most plaintiff lawyers would rather try cases in jurisdictions where there can be less than a majority vote for the verdict. I tried cases in a jurisdiction where a verdict could be returned 10 to 2. Many jurisdictions allow verdicts to be divided by a three-fourths vote of nine to three. In federal courts, all verdicts must be unanimous.

The Supreme Court, in recent years, has defined constitutional dimensions in both civil and criminal proceedings. The Court has sanctioned the use of less than twelve juries in both criminal and civil trials in state courts. State criminal convictions are constitutional even when not unanimous. The Court, for example, has upheld verdicts in state criminal cases that are 11 to 1 and 9 to 3. On the other hand, the Court has also set aside state criminal verdicts returned by five members with one juror dissenting. The Court has set aside a verdict in a state criminal case where only five jurors were used.

Federal rules require twelve person juries in criminal cases. They must be unanimous. The Supreme Court has found no constitutional violation in the use of less than twelve jurors in civil cases and has found the constitutional requirement that there be a cross section of people on the juries not diluted by the use of six person juries. Federal courts now have adopted a rule for civil cases allowing the selection of eight jurors, no more than two of whom may be excused during trial. If none are excused, all eight sit on the case without need to dismiss any as alternates.

I have set forth these rulings because of the continuing debate about whether smaller juries are as effective in rendering a fair verdict as are larger panels. Several studies have pursued this concern on a statistical basis. The Supreme Court acknowledged these studies and used them as support for drawing the constitutional line at six jurors rather than a smaller number. I think it important that lawyers weigh these factors in choosing the forum for their case.

The studies show that smaller juries provide less group deliberation. As the Supreme Court observed, this can lead to inaccurate fact finding and "incorrect application of the common sense of the community to the facts." It stands to reason that the fewer people deliberating, the less critical contribution can be made toward the overall conclusion. Studies show as well that the larger the group, the less likely that a single individual's bias will infect the deliberations.

The Court in *Ballew v. Georgia*, 435 U.S. 223 (1978), concluded that smaller groups of jurors produce less accurate results. Defendants in criminal cases with smaller juries experience the greatest harm. Smaller juries result in fewer hung juries. With a smaller number on the jury, there is greater likelihood of a person in the majority persuading others who might disagree to consider his or her viewpoint. Obviously, smaller panels are less likely to have minority members. Smaller sized juries usually result in smaller verdicts in civil cases. Although the Supreme Court approved the constitutionality of smaller juries in both civil and criminal cases in state courts and in civil cases in federal courts, lawyers should pay attention to these studies when considering effective persuasion in the use of juries.

CONCLUSION

Many attack the jury system on the notion that juries cannot understand complex factual situations. In cases where the issues are complex, the judge may assist the jury by carefully monitoring the lawyers' presentation of evidence, by careful instruction to the jury, and by judicious use of joinder of claims and parties. The judge can aid the litigants and the jury in complex cases. Nonetheless, the jury should be left to resolve issues of credibility that relate directly to its ultimate factual verdict. Stephen Alder authored a book called "The Jury." In doing so, he interviewed jurors from several civil and criminal trials. He concluded they had considered many irrelevant issues and "fail[ed] to see through the cheapest appeals to sympathy and hate, and generally botch[ed] the job." This kind of criticism is, in my judgment, totally misguided. Jurors are people. So are judges. People are not perfect. Our political process has always depended on the fallibility, recognized by most politicians, of the human being. Voter appeal is seldom based upon logic and rational thinking; it is based more often than not on voter prejudice (e.g. Willie Horton), and politically charged non-consequential issues. The court trial is, and must be, fundamentally different than the political process. At least we strive to make it so; yet, every judge, lawyer and student of the legal process knows that in dealing with people, whether the person is the judge, lawyer, witness or juror, the system is not infallible. But we continue to strive in the democratic process for justice by the best means available, knowing full well that "justice" may mean different results to different people with diverse interests and goals.

The people should never give up the jury system or succumb to superficial prejudices to dilute it. This is true even though there may be alleged imperfections in individual cases. Simply because someone disagrees with a jury verdict does not mean the verdict was wrong; it simply means if they had been on the jury they think they would have found the other way. When some people allege a verdict is wrong, it is important to consider their motives and interests. Everyone does not agree on the meaning of collected facts; even judges disagree on factual and legal significance. Why shouldn't jurors?

The jury system provides the ordinary citizen a direct means of participation in our government. It guarantees the ordinary and the extra-ordinary citizen will be judged by the people. The jury system belongs to the people. It is the best system mankind has devised to render justice. No other process affords the people access for equal justice. As the great French historian, Alex de Toqueville, observed:

"The jury teaches every man not to recoil before the responsibility of his own actions, and impresses him with that manly confidence without which no political virtue can exist. It invests each citizen with a kind of magistry; it makes them all feel the duties which they are bound to discharge towards society, and the part which they take in its government. By obliging men to turn their attention to other affairs than their own, it rubs off that private selfishness which is the rules of society."

CHAPTER VII
THE APPEAL

THE IMPORTANCE OF THE APPEAL
Playing At The Palace

THE DISCOURTEOUS COURT

LAWYERS SHOULD ALWAYS BE RESPECTFUL
The Rule In Lay's Case
The Tom Clark Story

PREASSIGNED CASES ON APPEAL

THE APPELLATE JUDGE IS HUMAN, TOO
The Politicalization Of The Law

THE CLIENT
The Cost Of Delay

ORAL ARGUMENT
Do Not Waive Oral Argument
Dress Neatly And Professionally
Be Prepared
Go Immediately To The Important Legal Issues
Visual Aids On Appeal

THE WRITTEN BRIEF
The Rule of "B–C–G": The Written Brief
"B": Be Brief
"C": Clarity
"G": Grace
The Understated Argument

THE IMPORTANCE OF THE APPEAL

A story is told that a young lawyer once told Chief Justice Taft that he thought that appellate work was not exciting because the real action took place in the trial court. The Chief Justice replied: "You are mistaken. The facts are on trial in the trial court. In the appeals court the law is on trial. This is where the action really is." There is no doubt the trial is more exciting than the appeal. More people interaction is involved. But what the Chief Justice had in mind was that all conduct in a common law system is governed by the law and the precedent of even one case can often affect the conduct of all citizens for years to come. Appellate judges are constantly aware of that fact. The lawyer in any case must initially convince the trier of fact that the facts are more favorable to his client than to the opponent. However, counsel is well aware or at least should be, that winning the appeal is essential to gain a victory for the client. It is indeed a hollow, frustrated and pyrrhic victory if the trial is won and the appeal is lost. So for the lawyer on either side of the case, the appeal assumes vital importance.

As a young lawyer I vividly recall arguing appeals before my state supreme court. I approached these oral arguments with a great deal of apprehension because of the responsibility involved. I also remember the several cases I argued to the federal court of appeals. I always felt in awe of the distinguished judges before whom I appeared on both the state and federal level. The formality and the exhibited scholarship the judges displayed added to the overall dignity of the proceedings. I still think back to those years to remind me that lawyers appearing before our court have a much different perspective of the appellate proceeding than the judge. I remember how nervous I felt as I argued each case on appeal. Because of those feelings I think it is imperative that appellate judges treat lawyers with courtesy and respect. When I hear appellate judges scathingly censure a lawyer in a case on appeal, I sense the judge may not have argued appellate cases before becoming a judge to appreciate how difficult a role it is for the lawyer in arguing the appeal for the client. Obviously in the rare case where the lawyer displays blatant disrespect for the court, there must be an appropriate judicial response. However, I do not understand judges who shout or chastise a lawyer with whom the judge might disagree. Judges who do that create a bad image not only for themselves, but for the entire court on which they sit.

Playing At The Palace

One time as an appellate judge when I was preparing for oral argument, I read a frivolous brief in a criminal case. I called the other two judges of my panel and suggested the case should be screened for no argument. We all agreed. Under our procedures, we notified counsel and offered him the right to object. Counsel wrote to the court and stated that he had some important information to give to the court and requested oral argument. We granted his request. Oral argument proceeded and counsel repeated the same arguments he had made in his written brief. I questioned him and asked if he had something else that he wanted to argue to the court other than what he had presented in the brief. He said "no." I then said the court considered his argument frivolous and that it was not necessary to hear from the government. After court was adjourned the judges were walking back through the hallway to our chambers and counsel approached us and suddenly moved in front of me. It startled me. (Today our security is such that free access to our chamber hallways is restricted). Counsel told us: "Your honor, when you have the chance to play the Palace, you play the Palace." I am confident that none of our judges and few lawyers view an appearance before the court of appeals as "playing at the palace," but the story does illustrate the importance of appearance, at least in the eyes of one lawyer, in the appellate court.

THE DISCOURTEOUS COURT

Sometimes, however, appellate courts can lend appearances which counsel may perceive as being discourteous. When I was first practicing law, the State Supreme Court was occupied by several elderly jurists. During most of the oral arguments at least four of the judges *appeared* to be asleep, two of the justices would generally carry on a continuous conversation with one another and appeared to be totally oblivious of the argument being made. No one would ask questions.

I like to tell the story of one of the old time, great lawyers of Nebraska, Seymour Smith, when he appeared before the Nebraska Supreme Court. He had obtained a large personal injury judgment that had attracted statewide attention. Shortly after his appellate argument we had him over to dinner one night. I said to him: "Seymour, how did your oral argument go before the Supreme Court?" He replied:

"Well, immediately after argument I walked out to the rotunda at the state house and, as you know, there is a bust of Abraham Lincoln out there. I stood in front of Abe and repeated my oral argument. I got a little more facial expression out of Abe than I did from the court."

LAWYERS SHOULD ALWAYS BE RESPECTFUL

In the early days of my practice, if you lost a case before the State Supreme Court, you had ten days in which to move for rehearing. You were given ten minutes in which to make oral argument on the petition for rehearing. One time an experienced lawyer lost his appeal. He felt the Supreme Court had ignored the facts and the law, so he filed a petition for rehearing. His written petition stated that behind the Supreme Court bench, carved in wood (it is still there) is the proverb that reads: "The Eyes and Ears are poor Witnesses if the Soul is Barbarous." Counsel told the court that it should put the quotation on the back wall facing the court so that the justices could read it. The Court struck his petition.

The Rule In Lay's Case

I once appealed a slip and fall case where the trial judge had directed a verdict against my client on the ground that my client had been guilty of contributory negligence as a matter of law. I thought existing case law made clear that the plaintiff's conduct was a question of fact under the state comparative negligence law. I felt fairly confident after my oral argument on appeal and thought the client would receive a new trial. To my surprise, the lower court's decision was affirmed. The court's opinion was difficult to comprehend; it read like a quite title action. Rather than deciding the case on the issue briefed, the court ruled that the plaintiff had failed to prove the exact place where the accident had happened. The court stated that all that was known was that the plaintiff had fallen on ice somewhere in a shopping center that was bounded by streets running north and west. The court had completely overlooked the testimony. In the petition for rehearing, I blew up all of the trial exhibits of photographs which showed the precise point where the accident had occurred. The issue was actually irrelevant. The company operating the shopping center, which was sued, maintained all the sidewalks and despite actual notice of other falls at the precise spot that morning, the managerial staff had done nothing to properly maintain the sloped, icy sidewalk. On the argument for rehearing, the judge who had written the opinion began to shout angrily at me. Why had my client stepped up on the sidewalk at the point where he had parked his car adjacent to a doctor's office? Why did he not use the crosswalk? This was a totally new and irrelevant issue. I tried to restrain myself. The Chief Justice let the argument go on for over a half an hour, despite its allotted time of ten minutes. I still remember I had tears in my eyes when I finished my presentation.

Nine months later I received a postcard; three dissents had been filed but the majority had overruled the petition for rehearing without opinion. I vowed never to take another appeal to that court unless I was absolutely required to do so. Several years later, younger justices were later appointed and the court became much improved. Shortly after my argument the court abolished all oral arguments on petitions for rehearing. One of the justices told me years later, with a smile on his face, that they always called the rule abolishing oral argument on petitions for rehearing the "Rule in Lay's case."

The Tom Clark Story

One of the more humorous incidents which occurred on our court when Justice Tom Clark, who sat with the Eighth Circuit Court of Appeals several times after leaving the Supreme Court, sat with me and another judge involved an employee of a company who was killed. The tragic events that led to the employee's death centered around his constant abuse of his wife. After one particularly intense domestic quarrel, the wife announced to the employee, "If I had a gun I would shoot you." He told her to wait a minute. He then walked into the bedroom, took out a gun from a dresser drawer, gave it to his wife and said, "Go ahead and shoot me." She did. He died as a result of the gunshot. The wife was convicted of manslaughter. Their five children were left without a father and, for all practical purposes, without a mother. She went to prison. The estate of the decedent brought suit against the employer's insurance company under a double indemnity accidental insurance policy. The district court ruled that the death was not accidental but was caused by the employee's willful conduct.

On appeal, the lawyer for the estate filed a very short brief, five pages long and, as I recall, without any legal citations. The insurance company's attorney was well prepared and cited many cases which seemed to support the district court's finding that the death was not accidental. At the close of the argument, the estate's lawyer stood and asked if he could have a moment to make a personal statement. I told him that the court had a full morning but that we would give him a few seconds to say what he wanted to say. He then stepped forward and stated, "I want the court to know that today is the proudest day of my life. I have never had the opportunity and privilege to argue a case before a Supreme Court Justice. Today I have the great personal privilege to argue a case before the Honorable Tom C. Clark, Associate Justice of the United States Supreme Court." He then added, "I am going home to tell my grandchildren that I was here and appeared before Justice Clark." When he concluded and stepped back, Justice Clark leaned over the bench and said to counsel, "I appreciate very much your remarks. I want you to know something. I am going home to tell my grandchildren that you were *here*." With that we concluded the morning session and we adjourned court. As I walked down the steps into the robing room, Justice Clark put his arm around me and said, "You know, Don, I think we ought to reverse that last case."

I assigned the case to myself. After considerable study, I became convinced the better reasoned cases required us to find the death was accidental and we awarded the insurance money to the estate. I have always jokingly cited that case to lawyers and law students as the most persuasive oral argument that I have every heard.

PREASSIGNED CASES ON APPEAL

Many state supreme courts preassign cases for writing the opinion on an alphabetical basis to a specific justice before oral argument. In other words, the justice who will write the case knows that he or she must thoroughly prepare the preassigned case before oral argument. Most federal courts of appeal do not preassign opinions for writing until after the voting conference. Proponents of preassigning cases argue that it allows the justices the benefit to divide up the preparation of cases. Obviously a judge will spend more time in preparation on the case when he is preassigned the case. I have always been bothered by a preassignment process. On most federal courts of appeal, each judge independently prepares each case and doesn't know who will write the opinion until after the voting conference. Each judge brings to the conference his or her own ideas and legal analysis. Thus, at the voting conference each judge makes an independent and diverse contribution. Under this system, the presiding judge of the panel generally assigns the opinions. The decision as to whom will be assigned a case turns on many factors such as the existing workload of the judges as well as weighing the degree of difficulty of other cases assigned to each judge. If a judge is undecided on a case, the presiding judge generally will assign the case to a judge who has stronger views representing the majority of the court. In my view, the biggest problem with preassigning cases is that the author judge who does the most in depth research can often persuade those who are less prepared. Other judges can read the preassigned memorandum and simply conclude: "This sounds ok to me." Thus the court may lose the critical independent insight of the nonauthor judges.

I recall an early case in my experience in the Nebraska Supreme Court where a condemnation award was overturned on appeal. The Chief Justice of the court wrote that the evidence did not support such a large award. A strong petition for rehearing was filed, citing the testimony of two expert witnesses who had testified that the value of the land actually exceeded the amount that the jury had awarded. Shortly after the opinion was filed the Chief Justice retired. A new Chief Justice was appointed. On rehearing the petition was granted. The new Chief Justice wrote a unanimous opinion vacating the earlier unanimous opinion and held that substantial evidence supported the verdict. My question has always been where were all the other justices the first time around? I doubt if this would have happened if the opinion had been assigned *after* argument such that each of the justices would have been better prepared at the voting conference.

THE APPELLATE JUDGE IS HUMAN, TOO

In a perfect world an appeal will be decided on the correct principle of controlling law. The problem with this approach is that the law needs to be applied to a set of variable facts. Justice Holmes' oft-quoted aphorism was: "Give me an abstract rule of law and I can decide the case either way." Applying facts to the law turns on two human variables: (1) the lawyer's interpretative application of the facts to the law; and (2) the judge's viewpoint as to the lawyer's interpretation. The success of counsel depends greatly upon his or her competence and quality of performance. Inexperienced counsel can often forfeit the right to address the merits of the appeal by failing to understand the controlling procedural or jurisdictional rules governing the appeal. This happened to me in a bench trial when I had appealed an adverse ruling of the trial court. The Supreme Court refused to review my appeal because I had failed to file a motion for new trial before the trial court. The court was right and I was wrong.

The other human variables affecting the success on appeal are, of course, the individual judges hearing the appeal. What is the judge's track record in life as well as in law? What are the judges' backgrounds—are they true scholars trying to apply rules of law or do they leave a paper trail of being result-oriented? What is their philosophy in life? Are they protective of individual rights? Do they have compassion for their fellow citizens? What kind of people are they? Do they have a reputation for being eccentric or senile? Are they predictable? Did they represent in their earlier practice corporate businesses or labor unions? Are they influenced by politics and politicians? In criminal cases are they pro-government? To assume that all appellate judges can shed the mantle of being a human being, shaped by their own background and experiences, is to assume a fanciful myth.

Jerome Frank, a noted judge, law teacher and author, once criticized Dean Roscoe Pound for defining law as "rules and principles." Frank noted that Justice Holmes had earlier indicated that rules and principles are simply influential arguments which guide judges to make decisions. He urged that "the decisions" that judges make are the law. Frank observed:

> And the honest judge. He, too, is often, quite honestly, "influenced by considerations outside the record." Suppose he is "bribed," but unconsciously by his own prejudices? The "pull" exercised on the crooked judge is often no more powerful than the "pull" which a strong bias exercises on a "straight" judge. And what of the honest stupid judge who misunderstands the rules which any well-trained law student believes to be clear, settled and easily comprehensible? Is stupidity in judges also to be labeled "abnormal" and therefore irrelevant to the study of law?

> Consider the honest intelligent judge who is tired and inattentive when an important witness is testifying. The writer well remembers that, as a junior counsel, it was his function, during a certain long trial, each afternoon to drop books on the table and scrape chairs on the court room floor in order to keep awake the judge who always lunched too well and was accordingly inattentive after the noon adjournment. A well-known judge, now retired from the bench, tells the

writer that he found it necessary at intervals to withdraw to his chambers, there to pour cold water over his wrists because his wits began wandering. 80 U. of Penn. L. Rev. 17, (1931).

The Politicalization Of The Law

The decisions made by judges are increasingly politicized because the decisions, although legal in nature, affect larger and larger segments of society. For example, laws dealing with religion or abortion often go far beyond traditional legal rules; whichever way the decision is made there are vast segments of society with strong views on either side of the issue. Appellate judges are no longer deciding simple cases as to whether a tort has been committed or whether a contract has been formed. We must often times decide legal questions relating to moral issues such as whether states may pass laws that disenfranchise a certain segment of society from employment or housing. Because of this philosophical challenge, the background of judges becomes even more germane to the lawyer who submits his case to an appellate tribunal. One administration and its attorney general openly advocated a "litmus test" in choosing federal judges. I once listened to a young member of the White House staff telling how this test worked and how judges of that administration were to be screened. One of my colleagues listening to the same lecture passed me a handwritten note that said they should put a sign around the staff member saying: "Beware; children at play". I mention this because notwithstanding every appellate judge's attempt to exercise his or her best legal judgment to a problem, lawyers should prepare their presentations in a manner that will be persuasive to the anticipated adverse viewpoint which certain judges might possess.

In expressing this belief no disrespect to any judge or to any court is intended. Nor do I intend to imply that an appeal is a game of Russian roulette. I simply state a fact of judicial life: decisions more often than not turn on the philosophical background of the people who hand them down. One of my fellow judges argues with me that it makes a world of difference whether an appointee to the federal bench is a Republican or a Democrat. I tend to be a little more of a purist, but, perhaps, more unrealistic. I respond that I think political philosophy is secondary to the fundamental concern as to whether the new judge has been *a good lawyer.* No doubt, we are both right. However a judge's philosophy is basic to his or her appellate decisions. The Supreme Court of the United States serves as the paradigm to such a theorem.

Compare the philosophical approach to government of Chief Justice John Marshall to that of Justice Tawny who wrote the *Dred Scott* decision. Or contrast the philosophies of Justices Brandeis and Holmes with that of Justice McReynolds, or more currently contrast the view points of Justices Brennan and Marshall with the opinions and views of Chief Justice Rehnquist and Justice Clarence Thomas. It should be obvious from this review that the philosophies about social, economics and political environment count immeasurably on how appellate judges decide cases. This does not and should not be construed to mean that decisions of the judges turn on their benevolent wisdom. The philosophical diversity of judges is what makes appellate courts responsive to varied and divergent interests of society as a whole. The human diversity of appellate judges is a mark of legitimacy given to the courts by the people. It is also what I tell law students makes the Supreme Court of the United States the greatest institution of government that man has ever conceived. But fundamental to the prophylaxis related to philosophical background of judges is the central point that most judges possess analytical skills and are students of the law who will attempt to decide cases on the record and the existing law.

THE CLIENT

There is another, almost forgotten person, who is important to the appeal: the client. The entire appeal process is generally considered too technical and left solely to the lawyers to handle. In my view, clients should play a more important role in the appeal. Clients seldom appear at the oral argument. It seems to me that clients should attend oral argument to hear the arguments and if necessary to consult with counsel. Clients should hear the questions the court asks counsel. Few clients seldom read the appellate briefs. I venture to say that clients would better understand the legal process governing their case if they had read the briefs and were present at the oral argument. Of even greater significance, clients should be fully advised and consulted on whether to appeal an adverse verdict or decision. Clients should understand that obtaining reversals on appeal is against heavy odds. Counsel should inform their clients that reversals are obtained in only about ten to twelve percent of the cases. Clients should understand that the trial court's rulings are seldom upset. Lawyers who are skilled in their profession can appraise the facts and law in light of the proceedings at the trial court level and predict as well as anyone the likelihood of a positive decision for their client on appeal. Lawyers should not be so blinded that they cannot perceive that the chances for reversal in most cases are very slim.

I recently sat on a week of cases in another circuit where we voted to affirm 24 out of 25 cases. Each of the judges expressed amazement at the number of non-meritorious appeals presented. I suspect in many of the cases attorney fees charged by counsel representing deep pocket interests were a motivating factor in bringing the appeal.

A few years ago we decided a negligence case against an insurance company who had appealed a verdict to our court. I was personally acquainted with the young lawyer for the company. He visited with me a few weeks later and told me that the insurance company had consulted a lawyer, in another city, who specialized in appellate work and who recommended taking the case to the Supreme Court of the United States. I told him that sounded rather foolish to me; that the Supreme Court was not going to be bothered with a routine negligence case. Any realistic appreciation of the limited resources of the Supreme Court should tell any lawyer that the court would not select a case that had no significant national concern. He said he agreed with me but that the other lawyer had told the company he felt certain the court would take the case. He said the lawyer had prepared the petition for certiorari and told the company that he had a foolproof system to get the court to grant certiorari. The lawyer always flew to Washington and made a personal appointment with the Clerk of the Court, where he would have the clerk review the galley proof of the petition and pick out obvious mistakes. He said in that way the clerk would remember the petition and would use his influence to have the court hear the case. I could not help but to chuckle out loud. I told him he and his company were "being taken." A few weeks later the court denied certiorari. Later, I saw the young lawyer again and asked him how much the lawyer had charged his company for filing the petition. He told me $4,800 plus the expense of flying to Washington. I told the young man he should tell his client to refuse to pay the fee and move for sanctions against the lawyer.

The Cost Of Delay

Over the years one of the primary concerns I have shared with other circuit judges is how to improve efficiency on the federal appeal court to avoid unreasonable delay in issuing opinions. As an attorney I once argued an appeal en banc for the Eighth Circuit. The issue was not complex. The only reason it was heard en banc was because three of the most senior judges had a dispute as to whether a writ of mandamus could be used to review a denial of a change of venue. I was quite certain the district judge's refusal to grant a motion for change of venue would be affirmed. Ultimately this occurred. However the case was assigned to a circuit judge who was very deliberate in his opinion writing and the opinion was not issued until over a year and one half after oral argument. In the meantime, we could not to proceed to trial until the opinion was issued. My client was in dire financial straights and finally took bankruptcy. We thereafter had no funds to prosecute his case and with the company in bankruptcy, our case did not have the potential for recovery of damage. We had to abandon the case. If there ever was truth to the axiom that "justice delayed, is denied" this was the epitome of such truth. In another case, shortly after I came on the court, one of the judges disagreed with the other two, but procrastinated as to whether to dissent or not. He finally concurred with the two of us. However this was two years after we had circulated the opinion to him. Let's face it, there are many lawyers who do not work efficiently and the same is true of a few judges.

I have never forgotten these incidents. I am inclined to think that judges who procrastinate in decision making have never experienced, first hand, as a lawyer what excessive delay can mean to a client.

The Judicial Conference of the United States has promulgated guidelines directing court of appeals to file opinions within 120 days of oral argument. Obviously, there may be good cause as to why this cannot be done in certain cases. Sometimes the court is waiting for a decision of the Supreme Court that may be pending at the same time on the same issue or perhaps the complexity of the case or the workload of the court justify extending the time limit involved. However where the court delays filing of an opinion for six or more months, because a single judge excessively delays the case to write a dissent or where the case is delayed because of poor work habits of the judge, there is no excuse.

What can the lawyer do when confronted with excessive delay in decision making, harmful to the client. The problem arises on both the district and circuit court level. Many lawyers are concerned addressing the judge or judges involved for fear that their expressed concern will cause irritation of the judge and perhaps bring about negative repercussions. However there are tactful means by which this can be done in writing to the judge or judges with notice to the other side. It has always been my belief that trial and appellate judges have sufficient integrity to accept in good faith respectful communication. Another avenue of approach is to notify the Chief Judge of the problem. I have never known this approach to bring about negative repercussions. One time a judge had an antitrust case pending before him for eleven years. He had repeated excuses for not trying it. Extensive discovery by both sides along with two interlocutory appeals had delayed the case. However, nothing had occurred in the case for over two years and both sides came to me as Chief Judge. I called the judge. I was concerned that the lawyers were about to jointly file a writ of mandamus. The day after my phone conversation the trial judge wrote that he felt he had too many other responsibilities to try the case and he was recusing himself from the trial. I immediately called another judge of the district who set the case down for immediate trial. After a three week trial the new judge handed down a decision and the case was settled.

Perhaps it is too easy for me to say, but I think every lawyer owes it to their client to notify the court the need for an expeditious decision where excessive delay is causing problems to the client.

ORAL ARGUMENT

Do Not Waive Oral Argument

My view as to the value of oral argument reflects the views of the majority of appellate judges with whom I have sat in the last thirty years. At the same time, there are many judges who disagree; some circuit judges do not feel oral argument is necessary to assist them in deciding cases. The dilemma the lawyer faces is how to accommodate the view of judges like myself and the view of those judges who feel oral argument is a waste of time. My response is simply to try to accommodate the judges who find value in oral argument. Counsel has more to lose by ignoring those who find oral argument helpful.

With the increase of volume in our federal courts of appeals' dockets, the circuit courts have had to reduce the time allotted for oral argument in many cases. With the limited time, it is important to get quickly to the heart of the issue. Often times, the judges will ask questions throughout the counsel's argument. One time when I was Chief Judge, an attorney wrote me a letter complaining that the court had been discourteous to him in oral argument because the judges occupied his entire argument time by asking questions. I responded by pointing out that the court must utilize oral argument in a manner to help the court to decide the case. He should not perceive this as being discourteous, but rather that he should be pleased that the court asked him questions since that gave him the opportunity to see what was bothering the judges. I explained that his written brief was well-done, but that the court needed to hear the helpful answers given by him and his opposing counsel.

It is impossible to schedule oral argument in over fifty to sixty percent of the cases, although all cases are reviewed on their procedural or substantive merits. In addition, many lawyers feel that once they have written their briefs, they have nothing more to say. As a result some lawyers waive oral argument. When this occurs, many circuit judges react as I do: that the counsel must feel that the case is not meritorious if he is willing to waive oral argument. It is rare for a case in which oral argument has been waived to be reversed. At least in my judgment, counsel for the appellant who waives oral argument is conceding defeat. In other words, the case will be affirmed. A lawyer who feels he has a good appeal in the case should object when he receives a notice that oral argument is to be waived. If the objection is overruled, then as appellant, it is likely that the court disagrees with you as to the merits of the appeal.

Why should counsel orally argue the case? There are several reasons, but one is worth mentioning here. Oral argument may be the only chance for counsel to try to persuade the court that the appeal has merit. Stated another way it is the one chance for counsel to find out what is bothering the court about the case. Some judges listen better than they read. The oral argument is the last chance the lawyers have to advocate their client's position before the judges vote in conference. Often, at the voting conference, judges on the panel observe that he or she had a different impression before oral argument but the argument changed their mind. Sometimes a judge will say, "I leaned one way before oral argument but now I am not so sure." Indeed, some judges feel a case should not be reversed without oral argument so the judge can be certain reversal is appropriate.

I recently sat with another circuit on an important insurance case. Based upon initial research I thought the district court was correct. I prepared a short summary order affirming the district court and passed it out to the other judges. Before argument commenced, the other judges all told me they concurred in my summary disposition. Because we had already scheduled oral argument, we decided to go ahead and hear the case. At oral argument, the appellant raised certain arguments that were not made clear in the briefs. At conference we changed our votes. Without oral argument, we would have reached the opposite decision, which in my view would have been wrong.

I once observed in a concurring opinion where the lawyers waived argument:

> Shortly before the scheduled argument in this case, the parties by and through their respective counsel stipulated to waive oral argument. No reasons were given. When lawyers agree to waive appellate argument, my initial thoughts are that (a) one party (generally the appellant) must feel there is little merit to the appeal, and (b) both counsel must feel that oral argument before the appellate court is not very meaningful. The latter rationalization surely misses its mark.

> This is not an ordinary case. It presents complex legal issues, with subtle and difficult questions. The issues relate to a narrow area of the law, unfamiliar terrain to some judges, like myself, in which we look forward to the aid and expertise of experienced counsel at oral argument. If the result here is in error (judges are fallible human beings), the lawyers and the parties may attribute it to our inability to totally perceive the significance of portions of the written record or to fully comprehend the law briefed. Many judges *listen* better than they read—at least I do. When oral argument is waived, the parties lose their only real opportunity to *excite* the minds and *sharpen* the legal reasoning of at least the two judges who will not undertake the same in-depth analysis and research as the judge who drafts the opinion. Waiving the opportunity for oral argument, in my judgment, is advocacy at its poorest level.

> Justice Frankfurter once said: "Every case worthy of an appeal is worthy of an argument." Sometimes when the case is patently not worthy of an appeal, this court will screen the case for "no argument." We do this not to save time for the court (oral argument takes little time for judges) but because

the court feels the issue does not merit oral argument. But the converse is generally true when, as here, the court sets the case on the argument calendar. Karl Llewellyn has observed:

> The brief can develop the frame; but the oral argument must get the case set into the desired frame, and for keeps. I do not see how so delicate a task can responsibly be left to paper when an accepted institutional pattern offers a way of dealing with the tribunal face to face.

K. Llewellyn, The Common Tradition: Deciding Appeals 240 (1960).[1]

We need to strive for excellence on appeal as well as in trial.

Dress Neatly And Professionally

It is not my purpose here to relate how a lawyer should make an effective argument. There are already enough books and speeches on the subject. I do make a couple of basic suggestions which can affect the judges hearing the appeal. Don't dress casually; be presentable and neat. An appeal is a dignified and formal proceeding. Sloppy appearance by counsel can be distracting to the court.

When I first went on the court, an unshaven lawyer with long hair appeared before us. He was sloppily dressed. I sat with two judges who were the eldest members of the court. The presiding judge looked down to the podium and in doing so he looked directly at the lawyer, who had a huge head of hair. I noticed he never took his eyes off the lawyer's hair. After argument I turned to him and jokingly said I noticed you

---

[1] Arthur T. Vanderbilt once reflected:

> The argument of an appeal is the climax of a case. . . . You face a select audience that is experienced, professionally critical but not unfriendly, and keenly interested in knowing the facts and applying the law to them and more or less prepared for the occasion. The challenge is great; the entire outcome of the case, victory or defeat, will be influenced by the effectiveness of your oral argument.

A. Vanderbilt, Forensic Persuasion, The 1950 John Randolph Tucker Memorial Lectures at Washington and Lee University 14-15 (1950).

were looking at the lawyer's hair. What did you think of that hair cut? He laughed and said, "I was watching it because I was afraid a bird was going to fly out of it."

Be Prepared

Second, be prepared. It is frustrating to the court if a lawyer is not familiar with the record and has failed to research and understand all of the controlling cases.

I single out two cases in my 30 years as an appellate judge which represent to me the best cases I ever heard argued. Each case turned on the extensive preparation counsel had undertaken prior to oral argument. One of the arguments was by a Legal Aid lawyer who was representing a class of social security recipients who had been denied benefits by the Secretary. The lawyer was poised and confident throughout her remarks. She exhibited remarkable knowledge of the facts and law throughout her argument. The impressive characteristic of her argument was the fact that she did it without any notes or briefs in front of her. Her sincerity was overwhelming, conveying to the court that a great injustice had been done to her clients.

In another case argued before our court in the late 1960s, I sat with then Judge Blackmun and Judge Floyd R. Gibson. The case was *Humble Oil Co. v. American Oil Co.*, 405 F.2d 803 (8th Cir. 1969). Humble Oil was the wholly owned subsidiary of Standard Oil of New Jersey. It brought suit attempting to dissolve or modify the 1937 injunction which had broken up the Standard Oil Monopoly. Standard Oil of New Jersey urged that they should be allowed to use the same trademarks as Standard Oil of Ohio because customers did not differentiate between the two marks. The case was highly complex. In attendance at oral argument were over 45 house counsel of both corporations. The record was voluminous. Appearing for Standard Oil of New Jersey was the litigation partner of Sullivan & Cromwell in New York. He had been a former New York State trial judge. His name was David W. Peck. Representing Standard Oil of Ohio was a leading lawyer of St. Louis, Richard Coburn. In the years that followed, I had occasion to tell both lawyers that their oral arguments were the best I have ever heard on the appellate court. Because of the importance of the case, our court provided each counsel one hour to argue. Judge Peck argued first. He did not use a note or read from any case or brief. He recounted by date and historical fact the background of the case. He then referred to the case law by name and page number. He answered every question without hesitation. His delivery manifested great confidence and sincerity. Coburn then followed and did the same thing. Both lawyers were on their feet for close to an hour. The experience was magical to me. If only every lawyer would prepare their case for oral argument on appeal the same way these two lawyers did, they would be much more effective and our role as appellate judges would be much easier.

Standard Oil of Ohio, which was the wholly owned subsidiary of American Oil Company, won the case. The injunction was not dissolved or modified. As a result of our decision, Standard Oil of New Jersey spent over eight million dollars the next few years in promoting a new trademark, now recognized all over the country as "Exxon."

Go Immediately To The Important Legal Issues

Finally, I would urge all lawyers to be themselves. Be sincere and candid with the court. Don't frustrate the court with jury speeches or read from your brief or argue collateral issues. Do not tell the court stories. Time for oral argument has been drastically reduced in all circuits. Get to the issues and try to answer without evasion of the questions the court asks.

I remember several years ago I was picking up my luggage at the St. Louis, Missouri airport. A young lawyer who I knew was on the same plane with me. He approached me and stated that he had never before argued a case before the court of appeal and was very apprehensive. He said he was not appearing before my panel and, in fact, was arguing a case against my former law partner. He was an able young man and very likeable. I told him the one suggestion that I make to most lawyers arguing the case for the first time is to go directly to the issues on the appeal. Begin your argument by outlining the legal issues and tell the court that you will assume the court is familiar with the facts and, if not, you will be glad to answer any questions. I told him the court is always well prepared and will have read the facts. The next day I ran into two of the judges that had heard that argument. One said to me that my former partner had argued a case before them the day before and that he had not done too well. He spent all of the time telling them the facts and never got around to arguing the issues before the court. The judge said the opposing young lawyer had done very well; that he had gone directly to the legal issues and didn't spend any time on the facts.

Visual Aids On Appeal

Lawyers who argue cases on appeal often mistakenly assume that judges have an extra sense of perception of what the case is about. The printed word often fails to visually describe complicated machinery, accident sites or the physical description of inanimate objects. Sometimes documentary evidence remains obscure without explanation. I have long urged lawyers to assist judges by bringing visual aids to oral argument.

In the days when courts of appeal heard patent cases counsel effectively used motion pictures to illustrate how machinery worked. In trademark cases, bringing in the competitive advertisements or objects of the mark can often aid the court. Blowups of contractual clauses can be of assistance to judges in understanding oral argument on issues of law. In an appeal involving the constitutionality of the Arkansas prison system, counsel effectively used a video display to graphically show the punitive and inhumane conditions of solitary confinement.

The one word of caution is: use a little common sense.

One time in a mail fraud case, a lawyer brought a blown-up map of the state of Missouri. The large map was mounted on a stand behind the podium. During the oral argument, however, the lawyer never referred to it. When he was finished, I asked him "just as a matter of curiosity, I am interested in the large blow up of the map of the state behind you. What is its purpose?" The lawyer sheepishly responded: "Well judge, I heard you speak to our bar one time and you suggested that we use visual aids in our oral argument to assist the court. I couldn't figure out how I could do this in this case so I thought I would bring in the map of the state simply to show you the small town where the defendant lived."

The first case I ever sat on in the Eighth Circuit was in September of 1966. I sat with the two senior judges of the circuit—Chief Judge Charles Vogel and Judge Martin Van Ousterhout, both great judges. As a lawyer, I had argued many cases before them, and I was understandably nervous on that day. Our first case was a complicated patent case. The lawyers were from large firms in Washington and New York. I read the briefs at least twice, and still did not understand the case. The lawyers did not spell out, except in technical terms, what purpose the patented device served. There was not in laymen's terms any description as to the device's use or purpose. Finally, as the appellant's counsel was ending his rebuttal argument, I realized that I could not continue to be ignorant—I needed to ask what I thought everyone would feel was a dumb question. With all the courage I could muster, I asked counsel: "Would you please tell me what the invention does? What is it for? What purpose does it serve?" Counsel apologized and said: "Certainly, your honor. It is a mold that is used to pour concrete for building a suspension bridge. The mold holds the wires together while the permanent suspension wires are being installed." All of a sudden the case took on a new meaning. Counsel used diagrammatic drawings to illustrate the practical utility of this "mesh of lines" that appeared in the brief. I felt very foolish in asking the question. We adjourned after the argument. I'll never forget how much Chief Judge Vogel put me at ease when he turned to me and said: "Don, I'm sure glad you asked that question because I didn't know either."

My point is that judges need assistance in understanding complicated issues of either law or fact. Counsel should never assume the court knows even the most elementary aspects of your case. Counsel should utilize whatever skills they have to help the court to understand the case just as counsel would try to aid jurors to understand the issues before the jury.

THE WRITTEN BRIEF

The Rule of "B-C-G": The Written Brief

Years ago I heard a lecture on how to write the brief on appeal that made a lot of sense to me. I apologize for not remembering the lecturer's name, but a truism is helpful whoever may have said it. The lecturer even provided an easy formula to help remember the elements of a good brief: "B-C-G." These letters provide a practical guide for writing a good written brief: (1) it should be *brief*, (2) it should possess *clarity*, and finally (3) the writer should use *grace* in writing it. These three basic ideas carry a great deal of common sense. I say common sense because these suggestions are not just techniques for brief writing, but rather are cognizable suggestions as to what will impress appellate judges who will decide the case on appeal.

CHAPTER VII — THE APPEAL

"B": Be Brief

Someone once suggested that if you want to be a good fisherman, you need to know what the fish want to bite on. The same goes for the appellate lawyers who want to persuade the judges before whom they argue. The more that lawyers understand the appellate process and the system under which appellate judges work, the better lawyers can achieve the means for presenting the appeal to the court. Lawyers should recognize what judges do to prepare for a week of appellate argument. The case the lawyer presents on appeal is perhaps one of thirty that will be heard by the court that week. To prepare for the week, each judge must read approximately thirty briefs and CURSORILY review the relevant parts of thirty records. Some briefs and many records can be very lengthy. Common sense should tell lawyers that the more they can inform the court in a clear persuasive style, written with as few words as possible, the more helpful and persuasive their presentation will be to the judges on the court.

The most effective brief that I have read was in a technical patent case which included a huge record. The trial had lasted over a period of three months. Despite an opening appellate brief which rambled for seventy-five pages the appellee brief was only fifteen pages long. To support the findings of the district court, the appellee has set forth the salient findings of the district court and in footnotes set forth the pages of the transcript which supported the findings. The law portion of the brief was short and concise, with no quotes, simply reminding the court of the basic controlling principles.

In writing a brief, lawyers should remember that they need not "reinvent the wheel." It is not necessary to fill pages of a brief with long quotes from older cases reciting well-known standards for summary judgment or the admissibility of evidence. Many judges make the same mistake in writing lengthy opinions. Chief Justice Burger once told several circuit court judges that if court of appeal opinions were longer than thirty-five pages, he just stopped reading. As circuit judges we all chuckled. We each wanted to respond that we used the same rule of thumb in reading Supreme Court opinions. But more to the point, lawyers should try to write concise and short briefs. When they do so, they stand a much better chance that judges will read their entire written argument and understand it in the beginning stages of preparing for oral argument. First impressions carry a great deal of weight.

"C": Clarity

Every book of style on writing will stress the need to make sentences of an appellate brief clear and to the point. The rambling sentence or paragraphs with double and triple thoughts leaves most readers confused. Years ago the *New Yorker* magazine satirically contained an editorial of an appellate judge opinion in which one sentence was 342 words long. Successful authors will urge ambitious writers to make their sentences clear and succinct. There is seldom an idea expressed in a paragraph of a written brief containing several sentences that could not be reduced to one or two sentences. There are seldom three paragraphs of a brief (or a judge's opinion) which could not be reduced to one paragraph. Of course this style of writing—one that is clear and succinct—requires more time for the writer. It is more difficult to write a short, concise thought.

I have taught a seminar at various law schools for several years. One of the exercises in the seminar requires the student to prepare a petition for certiorari for the United States Supreme Court. We study the purpose of the petition and emphasize that the petition is not a brief on the merits. The lawyer is simply trying to encourage the Supreme Court to spend its limited resources to hear the case. With almost 5,000 petitions a year, the Court hasn't much time to read the petition. One of the Supreme Court Justices told me once that it takes him "about a minute to read a petition for certiorari." I tell this story to emphasize to the students how important it is to make the petition clear and succinct as to WHY the court should hear their case. The clear and concise manner in which counsel states the proposition can often affect the success of the petition being granted. The same principles apply to lawyers writing the appellate brief.

Along the same lines, every lawyer should use understandable words. The judge does not have time to go to the dictionary to understand the brief. Words can and should be used in a colorful, persuasive style, but the sentence structure and wording should convey a clear message. Of course, some appellate judges are guilty of the same sin. When a judge tries to show his erudition by using complex words which send the reader to the dictionary, the opinion which should explain the law no longer serves to do so because the meaning is not clear.

CHAPTER VII — THE APPEAL

"G": Grace

Many lawyers lose their patience and feel that the opposing lawyer or the trial judge was so wrong that they must express their disgust to the reviewing court. Often an appellant's brief will begin by telling the appeals court that the opposing lawyer is so "stupid," or so "dumb" or just "plain crooked" that the merits need not be discussed. Often times briefs ridicule the intelligence of the trial judge. When briefs open this way, more often than not the reviewing judge will be prejudiced against the brief writer. A reviewing court will react in the same manner if the attorney misstates or misquotes the record. On a petition for rehearing, the petitioner was frustrated with the opinion of the Court of Appeals. In the petition, counsel foolishly wrote: "Presumably [the three judge panel] had a law clerk read a cold trial transcript. From this the panel concluded that the jury obviously did not know what it was doing, and substituted its findings of fact for that of the jury. That is patently wrong." The panel of judges was upset over the vituperative attack and reacted negatively to the petitioner. They even considered holding counsel in contempt. Briefs should never contain *de hominem* arguments challenging the personal integrity of the other lawyer or the trial judge.

A few years ago we heard a construction case involving claims of breach of contract with damages totalling several hundred thousand dollars. The trial judge decided the case without a jury. In the appellant's opening brief, I was surprised to find that counsel's first argument was that the trial judge had denied his client the seventh amendment right to trial by jury. The lawyer claimed that he had properly demanded in writing a trial by jury attached to his complaint. The plaintiff devoted the first ten pages of its brief to this argument. I immediately looked at the appellee brief. There was no response to the claim.

At oral argument, before counsel began to speak, I asked the question that had piqued my curiosity. What was the basis of his argument that plaintiff had been denied a jury trial? Counsel answered that the judge had usurped his client's right of trial by jury by having a bench trial. I said that I had looked all through the record, and I could not find any objection to the bench trial. I asked whether there had been a discussion at the pretrial conference about whether the case would be tried by a jury or the judge. Counsel responded that was the point of his argument—it was not in the record. I then asked whether there had been, in fact, such a pretrial conference. He answered: "we are confined to the record, judge, and it is not in the record." I again asked whether there had a been a discussion and whether in fact as counsel for the plaintiff he had waived a jury trial. He again responded that it was not in the record. At this time, I told him that I was *not* interested in the record at this point: what I wanted to know was whether such a discussion had taken place before the trial court. He then sheepishly said "yes". He then added "but, judge, it is not in the record." I told him that in the time remaining, if he still wanted to do so, he should address the merits of his appeal. The entire panel of judges was so disgusted with his response I doubt if any of us paid much attention to what he thereafter said. He was in bad faith with the court. I read his brief. His frivolous argument about the denial of the jury trial implied that his entire appeal was frivolous. The case was affirmed by a short order. The bottom line is to be truthful to the court. Do not try to be cute and cut corners.

The Understated Argument

There are various ways to make a point. If counsel becomes overly argumentative, his or her viewpoint becomes difficult to accept. An effective tool is to display a sense of fairness by recognizing that although your adversary makes a good point but to urge that further analysis shows that your adversary's argument should not control under the circumstance of the case. A little "touch of class" goes along way.

I am attaching as an Appendix an outline that I have given to lawyers and law students relating to the written appellate brief. I include the outline as a guide for lawyers in order to better assist the appellate judge. If you achieve that goal you will come a long way toward writing an effective brief.

APPENDIX

OUTLINE ON WRITTEN APPELLATE ADVOCACY

By: Judge Donald P. Lay
United States Circuit Judge
U.S. Court of Appeals for the Eighth Circuit

I. IMPORTANCE OF EFFECTIVE BRIEF WRITING.

A. Briefs introduce the case to the judges.

B. Appeals today are increasingly decided on the briefs.

1. Many cases are decided without oral argument; other cases are permitted only abbreviated argument.

2. Oral argument is used primarily to elaborate on points raised in the briefs and to address the court's particular concerns; many judges come to oral argument with deep seated convictions.

3. Justice Marshall wrote: "Regardless of the panel you get, the questions you get, or the answers you give, I maintain it is the brief that does the final job, if for no other reason than that opinions are often written several weeks and sometimes months after argument. The arguments, great as they may have been, are forgotten. In the seclusion of his chambers the judge has only the briefs and the law books. At that time your brief is your only spokesman."

Marshall, The Federal Appeal, in Counsel on Appeal 139, 146 (1968).

C. Judges work under time constraints and therefore the briefs must be organized and understandable.

1. A brief that is ineffectively organized and analytically obscure may jeopardize a meritorious appeal.

2. Less is usually more.

II. GENERAL.

    A. **There is no single way to write an effective brief; brief writing is a creative art.**

        1. A good brief writer should refine a broad concept take a novel approach, and rework his material.

III. MAJOR SECTIONS OF A BRIEF.

    A. **A brief must have a statement of issues.**

        1. The statement of issues should tell the court *exactly* what the appeal is about.

        2. The statement of issues should fairly state the legal issues in the case without excessive detail.

    B. **A brief must contain a statement of the case, which describes the proceedings below and includes a statement of the facts relevant to the issues raised on appeal.**

        1. Many judges view the statement of facts as the most important part of the brief.

        2. The statement of facts should be narrative and in chronological order.

        3. The statement of facts should be accurate and complete and should cite the record for support; lack of candor or omission of facts is improper.

        4. The statement of facts should not be overtly argumentative.

    C. **A brief should contain a summary of argument, which allows the judges to understand the thrust of the arguments in a nutshell .**

        1. The summary of argument should be short and concise.

D. **A brief must present the arguments, which show the court that a compelling opinion can be written in your favor.**

1. Only the strongest arguments should be presented; the stronger arguments should be presented before the weaker arguments.

2. Challenge the opposing party's arguments only *after* you have told the court why your client should prevail under applicable legal principles.

3. Break the argument section dcwn into logical and relatively short subsections.

4. A writer should always begin his or her argument by stating the applicable standard of review.

5. Apply caselaw to the facts so that the argument sounds authoritative rather than exotic or exploratory.

6. Adequately discuss a cited case to show why it is on point or analogous to the appeal.

7. Provide the policy behind a legal principle.

8. Provide the correct solution to the legal issue on appeal rather than merely attack the lower court's rulings or the opposing party's arguments.

9. Start the argument with a proposition the court must accept and then reason logically, step by step, to your conclusion.

10. Make a novel proposition seem familiar or at least a natural extension of established law.

IV. **A BRIEF SHOULD HAVE A SHORT CONCLUSION, WHICH STATES WITH SPECIFICITY THE RELIEF THE PARTY REQUESTS.**

V. ADDITIONAL POINTERS ON WRITING AN EFFECTIVE BRIEF.

A. The court should understand the entire case and the party's arguments after reading the brief.

B. The writer should adopt a tone of measured rationality.

   1. Too forceful a tone may make the court angry.

   2. Too forceful a tone may distract the court from perceiving the merit of the argument and may cause the court to distrust the writer.

   3. Appellate judges read briefs to gain information, not for exhilaration or excitement.

C. Be concrete and simplify whenever possible.

   1. Assume the court is unfamiliar with the record and case law.

   2. Recognize that judges are human and thus may not understand unnecessarily complex arguments.

D. Be persuasive—fit the cases into a logical, cogent analysis of the issue on appeal.

E. Write in plain language, clearly and precisely.

   1. Use familiar words and short sentences.

   2. Five to ten percent of the text can usually be trimmed without loss of meaning.

F. Avoid duplicity and demagoguery.

G. Use persuasive language—strong or weak depending on viewpoint.

   1. Lon Fuller, in his essay on the adversary system, writes that the task of the advocate "[i]s not to decide but to persuade. He is not expected to present the case in a colorless and detached manner, but in such a way that it will appear in that aspect most favorable to his client."

H. Personalize the parties or characters.

I. Do not refer to a party as appellant or appellee.

    1. Use section headings to alert the reader that a new point is about to be made.

J. Avoid multi-page quotations.

K. Cite cases and statutes in proper bluebook form.

L. Use active verbs.

M. Good legal writing requires accuracy in legal research.

    1. Be careful to cite cases accurately so they stand for the proposition for which they are cited.

    2. Cite all relevant cases—it is better to distinguish than to ignore.

N. Edit and proofread the brief.

O. Shepardize.

BIBLIOGRAPHY

Hoving, *The Art of the Appellate Brief*, 72 A.B.A. J. 52 (1986).

Lay, *The Crisis in Appellate Advocacy*, 16 Int'l Soc. of Barristers Q. 321 (1981).

Rubin, *What Appeals to the Court* (Book Review), 67 Tex. L. Rev. 225 (1988) (reviewing M. Tigar, *Federal Appeals: Jurisdiction and Practice* (1987)).

Samuelson, *Good Legal Writing: Of Orwell and Window Panes*, 46 U. Pitt. L. Rev. 149 (1984).

Sasso, *Anatomy of the Written Argument*, 15 A.B.A. Sec. Litigation 30 (1989).

Springer, *Some Suggestions on Preparing Briefs on the Merits in the Supreme Court of the United States*, 33 Cath. U.L. Rev. 593 (1984).

Wishingrad & Abrams, Book Review, 1981 Duke L.J. 1061 (1981) (reviewing G. Gopen, *Writing from a Legal Perspective* (1981)).

EPILOGUE

I finish where I started: I believe the practice of law is the greatest and most satisfying profession in the world. I have difficulty in perceiving how lawyers can become frustrated and disillusioned if they dedicate themselves to the reason the legal profession exists: to serve other people. Oliver Wendell Holmes once observed: ". . . all proceedings, like all rights, are really against people." *Tyler v. Judges of the Court of Representation*, 53 NE 812, 817 (Mass. 1900). The practice of law should not be goal oriented to material gain. The more attorneys focus upon financial gain for themselves, the more frustrated and less satisfying their professional experience will become. If the law practice becomes merely a business rather than a profession, the more the legal profession deserves the criticism which is now so prevalent. Many of the attacks made against the practice of law need to be examined. The self-serving interests of those who stand to gain by challenging a litigious America need strict scrutiny. The manufacturer who places an unsafe product into the stream of commerce, the physician who treats a broken leg when the patient has actually broken her hip, the employer who discriminates in its employment practices against the minority, the female employee and the older worker all have self interests to serve.

Without the lawyer to challenge wrong doing, we would exist in a society somewhat akin to one where law enforcement would be in absentia, and criminals could roam free to do as they wish. Equally significant to the welfare of society is the public interest lawyer who serves to deter state and federal governments from malfeasance. When the lawyers challenge the profit status of the wrongdoer it is understandable why they become the object of disrespect of both the public and private wrongdoer. This is not to say all of the criticism of the legal profession is frivolous; in fact, those who do challenge misconduct of the lawyer provide a deterrent to the frivolous lawsuit. The neutral judge and the jury must serve to maintain the proper balance.

Notwithstanding all of this, it is my judgment that the practice of law is indeed the most exciting, worthy and satisfying profession which exists. Where else can one attempt to challenge "the bad" to change to "the good." There is one caveat to all of this: this can only be true if our law schools and the profession itself are willing to concentrate on producing ethical, competent and effective lawyers. There is a great need for more ethical and competent lawyers. A disappointing news is that at the present time most law schools are experiencing an approximate one-third decrease in the application of aspiring law students. This is disappointing because there are so many of our citizens, particularly those within the poor and middle class, who cannot secure inexpensive legal assistance. Our legal aid clinics are taxed to the limit. There is dire need for lawyers who can assist others in avoiding hardship or injustice. There is a continuing need for lawyers to challenge traditional institutions to provide proper care and assistance to citizens who are rendered helpless by institutional indifference.

In the last four weeks I have just finished sitting on two different circuit courts of appeal, one on the East Coast and one on the West Coast. The diversity of conflict of significant legal interests in so many areas of life made me so much aware of the value of the adversarial system and the need for the competent lawyer to enable the courts to reach, to the best of their studied ability, the proper lawful result in all cases.

We heard appeals involving over a dozen immigration cases where diverse aliens were all seeking political asylum in the United States. Each alien presented a special family hardship and alleged possible persecution if they were to return to the country to which they had been deported. We heard tax cases, large and small, ranging in amount from a few thousand dollars to over $28 million. We heard complex cases relating to charges of malfeasance of agencies of the government of the United States, such as the Department of Transportation, Department of Agriculture, etc. Other appeals included challenges to jury verdicts for both employees and employers, where proper application of legal principles affecting age, race and gender discrimination in employment practices were raised. There were over a dozen bankruptcy cases, affecting individuals as well as large commercial institutions throughout the United States. There were appeals relating to the Employee Retirement Income Security Act of 1974 where individuals were seeking shares of pension funds allegedly wrongfully withheld by the trustees. There were tort cases of all kinds, claims over large commercial leases and at least a half dozen cases involving large banking institutions; there were numerous criminal cases involving serious crimes and allegations of deprivation of constitutional rights. We reviewed several cases relating to the Federal Sentencing Guidelines in terms of whether the district court properly sentenced individuals to the proper time limits. There were constitutional questions relating to the Commerce Clause, the First Amendment dealing with separation of church and state and free speech. The rights of labor unions and employers were involved in other cases. I could go on and on. My point is, the law is exciting. Without competent counsel these important rights of our society could not be properly determined by our courts. Competent counsel is so essential to enable the court to expeditiously and decide these complex cases. There is no other profession where individuals are inculcated in their schooling to promote the public welfare and to transform existing injustices in our society to assure that the legal interests of all citizens are protected. The lawyer possesses the most powerful tool to bring about needed change.

I have read where it is said that to be a successful lawyer one must be a liar or a cheat. This is hogwash! If you are "up-beat" on what the Constitution is dedicated to do, to form a more perfect Union, to provide equality before the law, to provide a system of justice for all, then you should be upbeat as to the legal profession. What society needs are more effective advocates who have courage to combat injustice. To achieve the latter, one must study throughout his or her life and understand the human process surrounding the law. Hopefully, this little book will provide some insight to young law students and beginning lawyers, which will help them to reach these desired goals.